# A Pictorial History of the Hamilton Workers

# ALL THAT OUR HANDS HAVE DONE

Heron,
Hoffmitz,
Roberts,
Storey

MOSAIC PRESS
'Publishers for Canadian Communities'
in association with
Office of Labour Studies
McMaster University

*Canadian Cataloguing in Publication Data*

Main entry under title:
All that our hands have done

Bibliography: p.
ISBN 0-88962-121-7

1. Labor and laboring classes - Ontario - Hamilton -
History - Pictorial works.   I. Heron, Craig.

HD8110.H352A55   305.5'6'0971352   C81-094140-6

Published by Mosaic Press, Box 1032, Oakville, Ontario, L6J 5E9, Canada.

Published with the assistance of the Canada Council and the Ontario Arts Council.

Copyright © Harry Waisglass and Wayne Roberts, in trust, 1981.

ISBN 0-88962-121-7

Typeset by Erin Graphics
Printed and bound by Webcom
Design by Doug Frank

# PREFACE

The McMaster Labour Studies Programme is pleased to present this historical study on work, workers, and worker organizations in Hamilton. This book is one of the visible results of the Programme's efforts, since 1976, "to encourage education, aimed at strengthening undergraduate and graduate programmes in the labour field, as well as non-degree programmes." With a wide scope of interests in labour matters, the Programme promotes interactions between teachers and researchers, scholars and practitioners.

The book is the result of two years' intensive research and collecting by the four authors. Dr. Wayne Roberts, our research director, and Mr. Shea Hoffmitz, our research assistant, initiated and co-ordinated overall development of the project. As the project grew in scope, two specialized researchers in the area of Hamilton labour history were enlisted. Mr. Craig Heron, a lecturer and doctoral student in history at Dalhousie University completing a thesis on Hamilton workers from 1895 to 1930, was involved almost from the start. Mr. Robert Storey, a doctoral student in sociology at the University of Toronto joined later and provided expertise on the complex developments leading up to 1946.

The authors searched the libraries and archives in Hamilton, Toronto, and Ottawa. To find a more complete photographic record of the wide range of occupations in the history of Canada's industrial heartland, they soon found it necessary to seek out the assistance of the people of Hamilton. They had the cooperation of many companies and local unions in digging through their files for old photos. And they had the enthusiastic support of many individuals who searched their homes and canvassed relatives and friends for photos. We are grateful to the companies, the unions, the archives, the libraries, and to the many people of Hamilton who helped the McMaster Labour Studies Programme assemble an impressive collection which will be helpful to researchers in the coming years.

This book will interest workers and employers, as well as students and teachers of Canada's social and economic history. Hopefully, it will enhance the appreciation for the importance of work and workers in the making of Canada, its wealth, its standard of living, its quality of life, its democratic institutions and its ideals of freedom and liberty.

Professor Harry J. Waisglass
Labour Studies Programme
McMaster University          December, 1980

# ACKNOWLEDGEMENTS

Labour history is a new field which requires new sources and new methods. Above all, it requires a new and more dynamic relationship with the people being studied.

In this project, we relied on the Hamilton labour movement and the community generally. We not only relied on them for photographs and interviews. We also tried to involve them as full participants in our book. Thus our debts are legion.

Our obligation and thanks to the many corporations, unions, and individuals who made this project possible are expressed in the photo credits section which brings the book to a close. Nevertheless, a few organizations and individuals deserve special thanks here. Dofasco and Superior Engravers Ltd. far exceeded the bounds of good public relations by opening their vaults of photographs for us and reproducing our selections. Jim and Isabel English, Harry Greenwood, Brian Henley, Jake Isbister, Elmer Moore, Ernie and Kathleen Morgan and Lloyd Bloom all became enthusiastic searchers on our behalf and made invaluable material available. Marc Zwelling did his best to teach us how to write for a popular audience. Finally, a special word of appreciation is due to the other members of the Labour Studies Programme who helped bring this project to publication, Marguerite Boux, Sandy Gage and Harry Waisglass.

Craig Heron
Shea Hoffmitz
Wayne Roberts
Robert Storey

December 1980

# INTRODUCTION

*Behold these massive towers of stone*
*In all their wondrous beauty.*
*Who builds those lovely marble towers,*
*Who works and makes the plan?*
*'Tis he who sleepless thinks for hours —*
*The honest workingman.*
*Ontario Workman,* 1873.

Over a hundred years have passed since this unknown labour poet sang the praises of the honest workingman. Yet those who worked and made the plan are still forgotten. Canadiana has become more and more fashionable, and these days coffee tables sag under stacks of weighty books about barns, mills, opera houses, train stations, and even outhouses. But the people who actually created these remnants of the past seldom find their way into the pages of these glossy volumes

Only in the last few years has a new generation of Canadian writers started to correct the blind spot in our appreciation of the Canadian past. They are now reminding us of our debt to the people who actually produced the country's wealth. We have begun to learn about the human costs of industrialization. We can now read about the efforts which working people devoted to creating a more democratic society in the face of fierce opposition from vested interests.

Labour history is a new field. It demands new methods, new sources, new questions, and new, mutual relations between researchers and their subjects. In this photographic history of Hamilton workers, we have tried to meet this challenge. We searched for that history in dusty attics and musty company vaults. We also jogged people's memories to help us piece together their history.

Historical photographs are windows on the past that can bring to life its vigorous dramas, cast fresh light on its dark recesses, and shed new perspectives on its overlooked experiences. A picture is worth a thousand words, the old saying goes. Photos can help us see things we might otherwise miss. In the more dramatic pictures, we can rediscover the excitement of an event in a way that words can seldom convey. Sifting through the many photos of the 1946 Hamilton steel strike, for example, helps us appreciate the emotions that surfaced in the weeks on the picket lines and gives us insights into the ingenuity and imagination of the strikers.

Many of the harsh indignities of workers' daily lives also leap out of these aging pictures. Long rows of women hard at work while a foreman glowers over their shoulders. Others tending chattering machinery with a naked light bulb glaring into their eyes. The state of technological development, the size of the machinery and the plant, the safety of production methods, the dirt and grime, and much more can all be "read" in many of the photographs we collected.

A keen eye can even spot some indicators of what workers thought about on the job. In one photo taken around 1910, for example, a row of pin-ups tacked up behind a worker's machine points to the image of women among some of Hamilton's male workers. In another, dating from 1919, Union Jacks strung betwen machines remind us of the power of patriotism. A 1941 picture of steelworkers defying an anti-strike law shows the same Union Jack being used to symbolize the justice of labour's cause. Photos of women workers during World War II indicate the pluck and pride of women as they reached out for new job possibilities. And, of course, family snapshots help us to remember that, despite hardships, working people found the time and spirit to enjoy themselves.

Pictures, then, can add a new dimension to our understanding of Canadian history. But can they give is a full, unbiased view of workers' lives in earlier times? Although the camera itself is a

mechanically neutral and accurate instrument, the photographer is not. Just as with more conventional forms of documentation, the camera can shape and distort our image of the past. Only when we understand how and why the camera was used can we come to terms with the range and focus, the limits and perspective, the problems and potential of this book.

In the early years of photography, technology determined what pictures could be taken. Until the 1880s, equipment was clumsy and split-second exposure was impossible. The photographer had to keep his subjects stationary and rigid. The workaday world simply moved too fast for these early picture-takers to capture it. Spontaneous snapshots of real-life situations became possible only in the early 1900s, when George Eastman's portable cameras began to reach a mass market.

Even when the equipment became more flexible, however, the photographer's personal inclinations continued to determine the way a camera's eye was focussed. Photographers had their reasons for choosing a subject, and they adjusted the angle of the lens, the lighting, and the pose to produce a particular effect. The results tell us as much about the tastes of

the photographer and his clients as they do about the subjects he recorded.

Portraits dominated the first years of photography. The camera actually democratized the portrait, which had previously been the preserve of the painter and his upper-class clientele. Commercial photographers, eager to capitalize on popular tastes, fitted up their studios with the Greek columns and draperies of traditional portraiture, and grouped their customers in highly stylized poses.The rarefied world of the studio reflected little of the rhythms of everyday life for working people, except to remind us that many artisans who posed for these portraits wanted the same symbols of respectability as the middle class.

The portrait has cast a long shadow over picture-taking. Self-consciousness in front of the camera encouraged by portrait work has all too often robbed a scene of vitality and spontaneity. Even when workers got their own cameras, snapshots often showed carefully posed family groups on special occasions. Likewise, when the labour movement began to produce well-illustrated papers in the 1940s, all too often rigid line-ups of executive officers stared stiffly at the camera's eye.

Man's fascination with the biggest, the

first, and the most spectacular helped to break through the stuffiness of the studio. From Victorian times, many cameramen tried to document a broader scope of social reality. Pioneer documentary photographs tried to capture the heroic and the spectacular. In a city like Hamilton, these pictures often featured activities involving workers, such as a grim fire brigade battling flames, or an army of workers setting new records of achievement on a massive construction project, or a colourful demonstration for labour's rights.

The postcard craze that flourished after 1900 specialized in scenic views for the tourist trade, but it also produced mementoes of gripping events, such as the destruction of a strike-bound company's property. Over time, this tradition in photography was incorporated into photo-journalism. By the 1930s, newspapers and magazines featured shots of strikes and other flashpoints in workers' lives. Photographers like Hamilton's Lloyd Bloom eventually amassed large portfolios of these dramatic pictures.

At the same time, other photographers began to look beyond the spectacular and to seek out more commonplace subjects. By the 1890s, one form of the group portrait featured workers in their own environment. The occasional travelling photographer convinced a factory owner to assemble his workers outside the back door of the shop for a group picture. Jean Beaudin's award-winning Canadian film, *J.A. Martin, photographe*, shows this kind of cameraman at work. In pictures of this sort, many details catch our eye — the workers' clothes, their age, perhaps their ethnicity. As well we might get some hints about their health, a glint of the stolid independence in their faces, and some signs of the playful comradeship among them. Certainly, these photos have a refreshing informality which is completely absent from studio portraits.

Many social critics also tried to use photography. Carrying the new portable equipment into streets, homes, and workshops, they sought to prod the public conscience and promote social change. In the early 1900s, public-spirited middle-class reformers turned the camera's eye on poverty and degradation, especially as it affected children.

Their strategy for reform shaped the way these pictures were composed. Working people usually appeared as pathetic creatures who needed a guiding hand. In Hamilton, the only signs of this kind of committed camera work which we found were some snapshots of Stelco smokestacks and nearby boarding houses taken in 1913 by Methodist and Presbyterian investigators. By the 1930s, however, social criticism had closer links to the labour movement, and the social realism of artists like Leonard Hutchinson avoided the condescension of the earlier reformers. Hutchinson's photographic studies of working people conveyed the dignity and strength of workers and their families.

Documentary camera work had another, less controversial form that came to be known as industrial photography. Early in the 1900s, businessmen, proud of their new factory equipment, sent photographers around the plant to create a visual record of production techniques for business journals or for the firm's promotional literature. Although these pictures often kept workers in the background — as servants of the heroic machine rather than masters of their own environment — they did convey much about working conditions. Industrial photographers were the only men to create an accurate graphic image of factory life, which was considered too ugly for refined tastes and too controversial for independent photographers.

Specialized firms like Hamilton's

Superior Engraving built up a remarkable expertise in industrial camera work. Eventually, some of the city's larger industrial firms, such as Stelco and Dofasco, developed photographic departments of their own, to preserve information for technical purposes and to illustrate the many company magazines which began to appear in the late 1930s. Occasionally, the work of these professionals showed similarities with the sensitive portraits of workers, produced by men like Hutchinson. Company pictures, however, glorified the accomplishments of workers as devoted and productive members of a large corporate "family", not as members of a downtrodden or heroic social class.

When workers themselves took pictures with their new Kodak cameras, they invariably concentrated on the happier moments of leisure time. The snapshot was supposed to preserve something special, to help rekindle the memory of good times and celebrations. The family camera seldom recorded unhappiness or the dreary, mundane aspects of work and daily life. Several of the company magazines which we examined borrowed from this form of photography and featured vignettes of men and women off the job, in order to promote employee morale and loyalty to the firm.

Of all the old photos which survived, therefore, only a few were produced by and for working people themselves. The preoccupations of commercial portrait-takers, middle class reformers, and company technocrats left great gaps in the photographic record of workers' lives. We had difficulty, for example, finding photos of residential communities in Hamilton (which probably appeared too plain and drab to merit much attention) or pictures of women's work in the home (which most often remained invisible to everyone but the women themselves).

Despite these deficiencies and distortions in the photographic record, we are convinced that the photographs that have survived are much more than interesting old artifacts. They are unique sources for enriching our understanding of workers' history. This book presents some of the most informative, representative, and dramatic photographs from among the hundreds we collected. For us, they are mainly avenues into the social history of working people. Yet we believe that a large number of the pictures here are examples of documentary photography which can stand alongside some of the best in the field.

To place the photographs in context, we have inserted a considerable amount of written material, much of it in the words of Hamilton citizens themselves. We have drawn upon old documents and newspapers, and on interviews taped over the past two years (available at the McMaster University Archives).

Naturally enough, the book reflects our approach to working class history. Instead of simply chronicling the battles of labour organizations, we wanted to lay the foundations for understanding these struggles as the product of everyday experiences in a rapidly changing industrial world. In the second section of the book, we carry the story of Hamilton's labour movement up to the tumultuous strikes of 1946. The climax of nearly 100 years of life and labour, these strikes marked the consolidation of industrial unionism and the dawn of a new age in industrial relations in the city.

We hope this book will take readers behind some closed doors in Canadian history and encourage people to learn more about the fascinations and lessons that history holds. A deeper understanding of "all that our hands have done" can help to develop a better idea of what remains to be overcome in the future.

# CONTENTS

**PART I: Life and Labour**

CRAFTSMEN

The Power To Work And Think   5

LABOURERS

Ninety Cents A Day   23

MASS PRODUCTION

Modern Times   33

WOMEN WORKERS

Bring Your Sisters   57

RECREATION

The Times We Used To Have   83

**PART II: A Union Town**

The Making Of A Union Town   103

Photo Credits   181

## 'We are Coming to take Possession of all that Our Hands Have Done'

I have builded your towns and cities,
    And over your widest streams
I have flung with a giant's ardour
    The web of strong steel beams.
I have carved out the busy highways
    That mark where your commerce reigns;
With hammer and forge and anvil
    I have wrought your golden gains.

+ + +

I see in the days before me
    My share of the things I've wrought;
See Justice no longer blinded,
    The weights of her scales unbought.
I see in the not far future
    The day when the worker's share
Is more than his belly's succour,
    Is more than a rag to wear.

I see on the morrow's mountains
    The glints of a golden dawn;
The dawn of a day fast coming
    When strivings and hates are gone.
Lo, out of the vastly darkness
    That fetters my limbs like steel
I can hear the swelling chorus
    That sings of the common weal.

For a thousand years you've driven —
    For a thousand years and one,
But I'm coming to take possession
    Of all that my hands have done.
And cities and towns and highways
    I've builded shall be my own;
And Labour, at last unfettered,
    Shall sit on the kingly throne.

Anonymous, *Industrial Banner*, September, 1911.

# PART I: Life and Labour

# CRAFTSMEN

Stonecutters, including future mayor Sam Lawrence (fourth from right in front row), photographed around 1913.

# The Power to Work and Think

Hamilton had only recently entered the factory age when an aging machinist took the stand at a local hearing to investigate the effects of industrialism. "I learned the whole art or mystery of mechanics — that is, so far as human skill, I suppose, could accomplish it," he told investigators for the royal commission in 1888. He could work with "either wood, iron, brass, blacksmithing, or anything; I am one of the old school." These were the words of an artisan, proud of his mastery of an entire trade.

The old-school artisan knew his trade as an art or mystery. By combining manual dexterity with informal and unschematized know-how, artisans held on to what one Hamilton printer defined as "the power to work and think." It was not a power which employers could undermine easily in the early stages of steampower and factories.

The far-ranging skills of the artisan laid the foundations of Hamilton's growth as an industrial city in the late nineteenth century. In the workshops and on construction sites, artisans used a few simple tools and their own know-how to cast an iron stove, set a page of copy for printing, roll a cigar, or build a brick wall.

Hamilton was renowned for its foundries and machine shops, and it bred a particularly hardy group of craftsmen who laboured in the sweat, smoke and grime of dark foundries. These men were proud of their trades and jealous of their knowledge. In the second half of the nineteenth century, they built up their trade union organizations to protect the standards of their craft. Early unions, in the foundries and elsewhere, developed constitutions and by-laws which specified the tools to be used on a job, the acceptable workload, the length of the working day, and the apprenticeship system for admission to the trade. By insisting that employers obey these rules, the early craft unionists hoped to exercise some authority in industry, protect their customary rates of work and pay, and prevent competition from poorly trained cheap labour.

Employers objected to these regulations as obstacles to their own power. Thus, conflict frequently erupted over who should set the rules in the workshops — the masters or the men. Over and above differences about wages and hours, this issue of control increasingly defined the terms of industrial conflict. The issue was not resolved in one strike or one year. It took 30 or 40 years, from the 1880s to the 1920s, before employers finally over-whelmed craft unionism in heavy industry. The corporations' power of wealth and size eventually overcame the artisans' power to work and think.

By the 1920s, the phase of Hamilton's industrialization that had granted a central role to the artisan passed into history. Self-operating machines replaced hand tools. Semi-skilled "green hands" took over much of the work which was once a relaxing portion of the artisans' routine. Highly skilled men worked on narrowly specialized tasks. As for the "art or mystery of mechanics," much of it was taken from the shop floor by engineers who worked directly for management and made all the planning decisions.

In their heyday, artisans enjoyed a special quality of working life and a special quality of social life. Throughout the late nineteenth century, the rugged independence of men who insisted on doing their jobs without management interference extended into the social and political life of the city. Off the job, gregarious craftsmen organized their own leisure activities, such as picnics, parades, or evening social gatherings known as "smokers." In the political arena, the deep faith of the early unionists in democracy and equality led to demands to root out monopolies and upper class privileges. These "uncommon common men," as one historian has called them, laid the foundations of the Hamilton labour movement.

## WIRE WEAVERS

A group of wire weavers proudly displayed the simple hand tools they used while working for the B. Greening Wire Company in the 1880s. In 1945, an old-timer who had started with the company in 1880 recalled that the plant "contained little machinery beyond a small wire rope closer, a couple of stranders, equipment for making clothes line wire and tools for forming wire specialties, and employed about 20 hands."

## ARM AND HAMMER

The village blacksmith was once a legendary figure in small towns across North America. In the pioneer horse and buggy age, no town could survive without his skills as a horseshoer gadget-maker and appliance manufacturer.

Hamilton factory owners remained just as dependent on the blacksmiths' thorough and horsesense knowledge of iron and steel. *Westinghouse Employees' Magazine* reported in July, 1945 that the

"...only Westinghouse blacksmith who ever shod horses is Tommy Bryson. He looked after army nags' foot troubles in the last war. Tom says he was glad to get back to the Westinghouse blacksmith shop where there are no horses but plenty of horsepower. Tons of equipment for giant Westinghouse electrical installations are fashioned in the blacksmith shop. This East Plant establishment resounds with the ring of steel as eighteen veteran smithies turn out high speed and machine tools for all departments, generator rings, cupola tanks, nuts, bolts, dirt collectors, air brake emergency bodies and many other articles... They're ready to make anything requiring brawn and precision. Anything but horseshoes."

## MACHINIST

Working in a forest of belts and pulleys, this machinist at Brown Bogg's foundry in 1913 produced industrial equipment without the aid of built-in precision equipment.

Unlike the artisans who traced their craft into antiquity, machinists were the new craftsmen of the industrial revolution. Indeed, they built the machines that powered the industrial revolution. One Hamilton machinist boasted in 1912 that "the industrial world depended for its success on the skill and technical knowledge of the machinist."

Although absolute precision was required in work on planers and lathes, no machinist could cope without a ready supply of intuition, tricks and deft touches that came "naturally" only after years of experience. Machinists with this background became increasingly important during World War I, when Hamilton firms retooled for war production.

## MOULDERS

A moulder's skill earned him many rights, but he never enjoyed a safe or clean workplace. One Hamilton moulder told a royal commission in 1910 that his shop was one of "the darkest and rottenest places in Hamilton, and so stuffy that you could hardly breathe." Moulders suffered from a high rate of respiratory disease.

In 1918, the smoke cleared long enough for this photograph of the Tallman brass foundry.

## SAND ARTIST

An old-style moulder pondered his next move in a small Hamilton foundry of the 1930s. By this time, only a few such foundries survived to recall the days when Hamilton was "the foundry city."

In the early 1900s, there were 18 foundries in Hamilton which employed hundreds of moulders. These men used the most primitive of tools at their workbench or on the sandy foundry floor, as they prepared sand moulds for molten iron, steel or brass.

The jobs he did were varied in the extreme," one veteran of those days recalled in the 1920s, "a single job sometimes entailing days of careful labour, and the work being given a finish in which the maker took pride."

The experienced moulder had a "sixth sense" for the qualities of sand and for the procedures of constructing a mould to produce a perfect casting from molten metal. His sixth sense, his painstaking attention to detail, his ability to blend elegance with utility earned him the title of "sand artist." The artistic quality of workmanship cherished by this breed of craftsman was resented by large foundry owners, who gradually developed machines to eliminate the need for moulders. Their work can now be prized only by antique collectors.

## CIGARMAKER

In 1910, when this photograph was taken, dozens of cigarmakers at the Tuckett Tobacco Company still fashioned "stogies" by hand.

Craftsmen producing consumer goods often relied on the goodwill of customers to buy union-made goods, and Hamilton's unionized cigarmakers were in the forefront of the movement for union label purchasing. Until 1918, when a long strike broke the local cigarmakers' union, Tuckett had a national reputation for union-made cigars.

## CUSTOM TRADE

This craftsman donned shirt and tie when he set out to work at Firth's special-order factory in 1946. Hamilton was a centre of the high-class clothing trade and its tailors took pride in the ancient obligation of their craft to design products which were both useful and attractive.

The arrival of the sewing machine in the 1850s threw Hamilton tailors into a panic. At first they tried to boycott the machine which destroyed their skill of hand-sewing. The skill required in custom-made clothing could not be replaced so easily however. Needle tradesmen adopted the sewing machine and used it to ease their task of producing a customer's suit of clothing. At the turn of the century, Hamilton was the third largest clothing manufacturing city in the country. Thousands of men and women made clothes in small workshops that predated full-scale factory production.

If the sewing machine did not triumph over the custom tailor, the mass market for cheap ready-made clothing did. By 1900, garments were no longer made by one tailor for one customer. They were mass produced by employers who carved up the tailor's work into a series of separate tasks that could be performed by lower-paid, semi-skilled workers. Under this new system, sometimes known as "the sweating system," men and women cut or stitched fractions of a garment. They became garment workers, not tailors. With this change in the trade, factory owners moved to small towns in Ontario and Quebec where they could gain access to a cheap, captive and docile labour force. Gradually, the number of Hamilton clothing shops declined. The few remaining firms tended to specialize in the manufacture of high-quality clothing.

## BRICKLAYERS

Trowels and wheelbarrows were the heavy equipment provided for bricklayers at Slater's new mill in 1900.

Bricklayers wielded their trowels, mortar and bricks in a way which seemed so simple. But no contractor, architect or engineer could manage to reduce the bricklayers' skill level or subdivide their work so that semi-skilled men could replace them. Bricklayers reigned supreme as the "aristocracy of the building trades" until pre-cast cement developed as a substitute for bricks and blocks.

## ART AND PRESERVATIVES

The printer and "printer's devil" in this photo worked at the case producing the Hamilton *Labor News* in 1914.

Each printer had a style of his own as he juggled type from the case and set it on a stick. It was a job that involved mind and body, that demanded judgement and agility.

Printers regarded their work as sacred — they had, after all, brought literacy to the world — and referred to their shops as "chapels." They were not just typesetters; they were creative masters of "the art preservative of arts." Their craft, like other artisanal crafts, had "mysteries," which printers kept to themselves and passed on to apprentices or "printer's devils." In strong union shops, even foremen had to join the union, and non-union supervisors were barred from the composing room.

"Red-Ink," a Hamilton printer of the 1880s, compiled a book about printers just as the typesetting machine was coming into use, challenging the "quaint conceits and eccentricities" of the old-style "typo." Red Ink had heard of all the advantages offered by these machines:

It'll set the type quite neatly, at a most tremendous speed,
And the clever printer man, they say, we shall no longer need.
A million ems, or more, a day, they say it will turn out,
Correct its proof, revise, make-up, and whirl the forms about;
Deliver papers in the street, and do it mighty quick,
And the most admired thing of all — "the beastly thing don't kick!"

## TRADE SCHOOL

Schoolboys tried their hands at woodworking in one of Canada's first technical schools, the Hamilton Technical School, in 1909.

The scheme had been promoted by businessmen, who preferred a publicly financed training system to the traditional apprenticeship system. Previously, apprentices spent up to six years acquiring on-the-job training while earning a wage from their bosses.

The apprenticeship system had been the bedrock of union control in a trade. It allowed craftsmen to control the numbers entering a trade by insisting on a certain ratio of apprentices to journeymen (skilled craftsmen). It allowed the union to supervise the training of apprentices and thus guard trade mysteries within their own ranks.

The system broke down when employers began treating apprentices as cheap labour rather than trainees. Employers then faced a problem of their own making — where would they get skilled men with the general training that was still needed? Technical schools were supposed to provide the answer. By 1919, the principal of the Hamilton Technical School claimed it was "one of Hamilton's most important industries... producing skilled workers with which to promote the industrial welfare of the city."

## HOUSE IN A DAY

August 14, 1913, as building tradesmen raced against time to complete a house in one day.

The stunt had been sponsored by a local contractor, James Bryers, as his contribution to Hamilton's centennial celebrations. The feat captured world-wide attention and shocked everyone with its challenge to customary notions of time on the job.

At first, craftsmen in the building trades were outraged by the plan and convinced the Hamilton Trades and Labor Council to pass a resolution of protest against "a speeding system in the building trade." "Realizing that no house fit for habitation can be erected in any such time this Council records its entire hostility to such a performance as calculated to create a false impression of a fair day's work besides endangering the lives of workingmen employed on the same." The bricklayers' union threatened fines of $50 for any member participating in the project.

Eventually Bryers agreed to hire only union labourers. They broke all previous records and built the house in one day. When the celebration died down, earlier union concern about "beat the clock" methods of construction proved justified. On August 15, the *Herald* editorialized: "Now that it has been demonstrated that a house can be built in a day, dilatory contractors won't have a leg to stand on when people complain."

## THE OLD PATTERN

This patternmaker puffed on his cigar while taking a final check on his measurements. He was chalking up heavy metal for torch cutting at Sawyer Massey in 1944. More refined work demanded the use of micrometers to measure metal down to one-thousandth of an inch for a cut-line.

Patternmakers or template makers who commanded these skills did not need to look over their shoulders for a foreman. They carried out the executive and manual tasks of their trade with the classic independence of the artisan.

Although artisans and their craft unions were excluded from heavy industry after 1920, elements of the craft tradition survived. Skilled workers in modern factories often played a leading role in the rise of industrial unions, which organized all workers regardless of craft. Jim Stowe, a patternmaker at Canada Iron during World War II, helped organize a Steelworkers' local there. Stowe was president of the Hamilton Labor Council throughout the period of industrial union organizing that climaxed in the strikes of 1946.

## WELDER

The old bowler hat has been replaced by a baseball cap and the old skills of the artisan have been replaced by the new skills of the welder at Slater Steel in the 1940s. Although many new skills were created within factory walls, specialty tradesmen were rarely allowed the independence of mind and judgement that had defined the artisanal style of work.

## HIGH WIRE ARTIST

Balanced on a high-wire, an electrician overlooked the city created by new industries and new energies. He was photographed in 1916.

Electrical appliances were the showpieces of the new household and industrial technology, and electricians were the tradesmen who carried out the conversion. Though born into the "new" age, electricians quickly developed all the forms and customs of older crafts. Through well-organized unions they jealously guarded rules for work in their trade.

# LABOURERS

An Italian labourer repairing the roadbed of the
Hamilton Street Railway in 1907.

# Ninety Cents a Day

Labourers were the muscle-men of the Hamilton working class. In construction, they dug with picks and shovels to lay the foundations for a building, sidewalk or road. In factories, they pushed materials around in wheelbarrows or shoved giant castings along the floor to their destination. As long as there was plenty of cheap human labour around, employers saw no need to mechanize. Only at the turn of the century did cranes and steam shovels begin to replace the labourers' muscle-power.

Most labourers were immigrants. During the nineteenth century they were often desperate refugees from the Irish famines, our first "boat people." After 1900, a land crisis in southern and eastern Europe sent another wave of recruits to the civilian army that built Canada's roads and factories. These newcomers, lacking industrial and language skills and with few community resources to fall back on, were shunted into the heaviest and dirtiest jobs that native Canadians refused to take.

Security was beyond the reach of the hardest working labourer. Labourers were hired on a temporary basis, as "casual labourers." In Hamilton, a foreman might take on some men to unload a boxcar or move some scrap. A few days later, they would be tramping the streets again in search of work, or heading north to the mine and lumber camps, or hopping a train west for the fall harvest. All labourers were part of this continent-wide "floating" labour market, forced to move on with each boom and bust of the industrial frontier.

Labourers lived on the brink of economic disaster. Most of their jobs were at best seasonal and the long winter months meant prolonged unemployment, with only the meagre savings from the summer to tide over the labourer and his family. And then there were the winter years of life — most labouring jobs demanded husky, young men, and left aging workers worn out and penniless. According to the editor of the Hamilton *Herald* in 1914, even those fortunate enough to work for the Hamilton city government could barely survive.

"Is 22 cents an hour enough to pay a robust, industrious man for doing hard manual work? Possibly a frugal, thrifty man could support a family decently on that pay if he were to get steady work all year. But corporation [city] labourers do not get steady work. They average about eight months' work in the year, and even the steadiest worker will not be able to put in more than 50 hours a week. Not many of them can make as much as $400 a year. Can a man support a family in decency on an income of $400 a year at the present time? Fully a third of his income must go for rent, leaving not much more than $250 for food, clothing, and fuel. Economize as thriftily as they may, the breadwinner and his wife who have no more than this sum to spend must find it hard to provide the necessities of life for themselves and their children."

Labourers seldom maintained permanent organizations to fight for better wages and working conditions. They drew some collective strength from the ethnic traditions which they brought with them from their homelands. But this cultural heritage could just as easily divide ethnic groups and hamper the efforts of labour organizers.

In 1885 R.A. Langlois lamented the fate of the Hamilton labourer in a poem he composed for a workingmen's picnic:

*We are off to our daily work,*
  *On the Hamilton corporation;*
*To pick and shovel the dirt*
  *Is our constant occupation.*
*Others as well as myself,*
  *In the city service have grown gray —*
*And now in our old age*
  *We get but ninety cents a day.*


*Oh! but we'll soon be rich!*
  *You bet, and in our carriages ride,*
*For on such magnificent salary,*
  *We can throw dull care aside.*
*With our extensive "bank" account*
  *To creditors we can truthfully say —*
*We are full-fledged, bloomin' aristocrats*
  *On our ninety cents a day.*


*But we are digging and shovelling dirt*
  *That's where the truth comes in,*
*And to be honest on ninety cents a day,*
  *The bank account must be thin.*
*God help our families at home,*
  *Is what we often say,*
*They are kept half-starved and half-naked*
  *On our ninety cents a day.*

## DOWN BELOW
With their bare hands and the most basic of tools, this crew gouged out a tunnel along Hunter Street for the Toronto, Hamilton and Buffalo Railway. It was one of the most massive and well-publicized construction feats of the 1890s.

Cochran Photo

## THE LONG HAUL
Workers raised a telephone pole the hard way, in the early days of this century.

## WRECKING CREW

A wrecking crew tore apart the old James Street Incline Railway building in 1947. Even at this late date, backbreaking labour remained the rule in construction.

## WHITEWINGS

In wintertime, blizzards snarled up city streets until labourers shovelled them clear. The joys of the job were dear to men such as "Whitewings," whose cheery exploits were recorded by the *Spectator* in 1909.

"He is set to work shovelling snow on the main streets. At the curb the snow is soft and covers nearly four inches of chilly water. The water soaks through his heavy shoes, or the hole in his boots, where his youngest child nailed him to the floor as a joke on father. His mitts also become soaked, and he puts them into his pocket.

"Traffic awakens and a sleigh passes. The driver, in high good humor, nearly catches Whitewings between a telegraph pole and the rear bobs of the sleigh. You can imagine him singing at his work, a merrey roundelay. He stops to say things to the driver.

"Finally the sleighs arrive which are to cart the piles of snow to the side streets. Into these sleighs Whitewings shovels his pile of frozen slush. In the work of elevating his shovel to cast the beautiful over the side of the sleigh, much water runs up the handle and continues on its way up his sleeve. At this joke he laughs heartily. The sleigh filled, he follows it to the unloading point, where, assisted by others of his kind, all as jocular as he, he again seized his shovel and levels the snow over the roadway. He is then at liberty to return to his home, where hot beverages prevent him from dying before the end of the day. His clothing is put in the oven to cook, and his day's work is over. Verily, a life of idle luxury!"

# MASS PRODUCTION

A solitary worker stood before an industrial cathedral, a cold rolling machine at Dofasco, in the 1940s.

# Modern Times

Hamilton had once been known as "the Birmingham of Canada," a small city where people worked in small locally-owned mills, shops and foundries. By the 1920s, the fiery mills of the Steel Company of Canada, Dominion Foundries and Steel and other huge metal-working firms changed the face of the city and its workforce. Hamilton became "the Pittsburgh of Canada." Its workforce entered into "Modern Times," an age immortalized by Charlie Chaplin's scramble with grotesquely overpowering machines and autocratic managers.

In the new Hamilton, business life was dominated by large corporations, each controlling enormous assets and hiring thousands of workers. Local industrial giants, like the Steel Company formed in 1910, gobbled up harbour space alongside expanding branch plants of multinational corporations such as International Harvester. These corporations were not subject to the informal control of a community, to the union label campaign of the labour movement or the power of any one group of craftsmen. They were run by absentee owners, oriented to far-away markets and built with the labour of countless skills and men.

Inside these factories, new production techniques disrupted older patterns of work for both artisans and labourers. Craftsmen were confronted with devices that eliminated the need for their manual and judgemental skills. In the new regime, machines could run without men and manufacturers took special joy in announcing the new terms of employment. This is how one business journal rubbed in the significance of its machines to replace moulders:

"The moulding machine is purely and simply a mechanical moulder and differing from its human competitor can work the whole twenty-four hours without stopping, knows no distinction between Sundays, holidays and any ordinary day, requires as its only lubricant a little oil, being in fact abstinent in all other matters, has no near relatives dying at awkward moments, has no athletic propensities, belongs to no labor organization, knows nothing about limitation of output, never thinks of wasting its owner's time in conversation with its fellow machines. Wars, rumors of war, baseball scores, have no interest for it and its only ambition in life is to do the best possible work in the greatest possible quantity."

The work of labourers was also taken over by superhuman equipment. In the era of mass production, automatic belts and conveyors rather than labourers with wheelbarrows moved parts though the stages of production. The assembly line, not brute strength, came to define the tasks of labourers.

New concepts of management took hold. Decisions were made by centralized planning and engineering staff in the front office, not by production workers on the shop floor. The more skilled jobs were divided into precise tasks, which were then parcelled out to semi-skilled machine-tenders. New classes of "semi-skilled" workers began to emerge — men and women who were limited to one specialized assignment. These new factory workers had to follow their bosses' strict instructions about the way work was to be done, and were excluded from the informal, on-the-job reckoning of the old days.

It was the era of "scientific management." New machines and more aggressive managers tried to speed-up the work process by reducing the amount of control workers had over their jobs. Managers kept closer tabs on their workers, and sometimes sent special inspectors around to take precise time measurements of each job. Management insistence on total control of the work process led inevitably to wholesale attacks on unions, many of which had been tolerated in an earlier era of small shops and hand tools. Unions might have served as some countervailing force to managers' monopoly over all decisions, but by 1920 most unions were expelled from heavy industry.

Factory workers' resentment of management autocracy ran deep. But until the 1940s, when workers established industrial unions to re-assert their human rights on the job, protest had to be anonymous, as was this poem published by the Hamilton *Labor News* in 1915. Entitled "Efficiency Expert in Hell," it expressed widespread feelings about the unholy directions of "modern times."

*The devil opened a furnace door*
*And heaved in a shovel of coal,*
*When out there popped on the scorching floor*
*A truculent, half-naked soul.*

*"Look here, good devil," it said, "I pray*
*You will pardon my seeming haste.*
*I am — you must listen to what I say —*
*Appalled at your awful waste!*

*Two-thirds of your heat goes up the flue,*
*Your coal is but half-consumed;*
*If a modern plant should compete with you*
*This business were surely doomed.*

*Your times and motions I've studied well*
*As you hustle the sinners in,*
*And I find you have here but a third-rate hell*
*And the way it is run is a sin!"*

*If you stay down here you will get my job!"*
*(Here he uttered a dismal groan)*
*"But if you go on (here he gave a sob)*
*"You will fix up a hell of your own."*

*The devil grabbed up that critic then*
*With an angry shake and a flirt,*
*And said: "Go back to the world of men*
*You efficiency expert.*

## THE RIGHT WAY

Two workers guided a riveter along its path at National Steel Car around 1913. Prior to the development of hoists and cranes, gangs of heavy-set labourers lugged unfinished projects from machine to machine.

By 1913, crane operators swung tools and assembly parts to their destinations. A visitor to National Steel Car marvelled at the changes wrought by this mechanization: "It is impossible to form an idea of how much labour is saved by the use of these hoists. They pick up sides of the cars and place them in position, the workmen being only required to operate the portable riveter and secure the car in place."

But a different story, recalling those same "old days," came in 1943 from National Steel Car's own magazine, *The Car Builder*. "Pete still has a hernia he developed handling oak end sills," and Mike "bears a brand of the old days in a badly mutilated hand from an accident while operating his pet machines... We worked an average of twelve hours a day seven days a week then."

The newly-designed power machinery did not pause to see if all hands were clear before compressing a rivet or swinging blindly along overhead track. This photograph was taken to illustrate the care necessary in handling such dangerous devices.

## CHILD LABOUR

These young girls barely had time to raise their eyes for a photographer as they packaged plug tobacco at Tuckett's around 1910. They knew that child labour was not limited to the England of Charles Dickens' day. Children were an important source of cheap labour for Hamilton employers until the 1920s.

In 1888, a royal commission heard testimony from two of the nearly 150 boys and girls who worked at the Tuckett Tobacco Company as "stemmers," earning $3 to $5 a week — less than half the adult male wage. Although provincial legislation required children to stay in school until the age of 14, one lad admitted that he had started work at age ten.

Reformers, including labour leaders, believed that children belonged in school. By 1919 they convinced the Ontario government to raise the school-leaving age to sixteen. This legislation caused some difficulties for parents who needed the extra income from a working son or daughter to help pay the family bills. One angry Hamilton mother complained that "Education is a fine thing, but it does not fill the stomach."

**NO BOTTLENECKS**
This quality control worker took a back seat to the machine as he eyed the bottles that were whisked by him in the 1930s.

## ON THE LINE

No eyes strayed from the work directly before them as Remington Rand assembly workers paid heed to the poster demanding "Silence to Prevail in this Department." The photograph was taken in 1947.

Conversation was subversive to the efficiency of modern factories. Co-ordination not co-operation of labour was the ideal. Since all planning decisions were made at front office, there was no need for production workers to exchange ideas and opinions on company time. Despite the large numbers of workers massed together in these factories, work ceased to be a collective human process.

**HARD PRESSED**
Rows of workers fed metal to punch presses under
the exacting scrutiny of mechanical counters that
monitored productivity at Wallace Barnes in 1942.

## THE TREADMILL

On the opening day of Hamilton's Firestone plant in 1922, a total of 55 tires were hand-made and cured by about 150 employees. As depicted in this photograph, the tires were built on donut-shaped steel cores atop spoke-framed "clincher" machines.

Bill Fry, who worked at the plant in those early days of 10½ hour shifts, six days a week, recalls that the ingredients for tires were prepared on another floor level. The rubber, oils, sulphur and carbon lamp blacks were mixed in vats, then sent by chute onto the mill lines and calender machine. There, cotton fabric was bonded to a coating of rubber, pressed between large rollers, then cut into plies on a bias.

Tire building required detailed hand work. Two plies were cemented and stitched down on the steel core. Then wire beads were applied and two more plies were added. Finally tread and sidewall were stitched down, again by hand.

## TIRE BUILDERS

"Tire builders are born, not made," insisted one former Firestone employee, who took pride in the individual "touch" that went into the building of each tire. Machine-made tires were still a generation away when this photograph was taken in 1922, and regular employees could easily distinguish between the handiwork of "Bill's tire" or "Tom's tire."

The talent and judgement of tirebuilders determined output in the plant, so management instituted a host of efficiency schemes to speed up the men. "The guts of the union came from the tireroom," where workers needed protection from the harassment of "the rateman" and his time-study charts, claims veteran Firestone unionist Harold Keeton.

## MEN OF STEEL

This rugged crew at Hamilton Steel and Iron's rolling mill took a break for company identification in 1906. Within four years, a succession of mergers culminated in the formation of the giant Steel Company of Canada.

From the beginning, the Hamilton steelworker was dwarfed by massive technology and corporate power. Yet the human element remained at the centre of steel production. Radios and cars were assembled, food and tobacco were processed, but steel was produced. Production was timed by frenzied bursts of strenuous exertion, not by regular rhythms of a conveyor belt. Steelworkers operated in a milieu of self-discipline, not machine discipline. Quick judgement and close teamwork were required at every stage.

Thus, steelmaking produced its own style of industrial relations. The pendulum swung precariously, between iron-fisted supervisors and self-directed workers.

## GATES OF HELL

Carmen Ciancone still remembers the excitement of his first day at the open hearth in the late 1920s. It was "like entering another world." His senses were bombarded with wailing sirens, charging cranes and black clouds of smoke spewing out from locomotives. Men joined in pitched battle against dust and molten steel.

In the open hearth, the iron from the blast furnace was poured into the top, then cooked with the aid of fuel and blowing oxygen at temperatures of 3000 degrees Fahrenheit until the "heat" was ready to be "tapped." As the steel cooked, workers added refining agents, as in this photo at Stelco in 1942.

This process, known as making back or front wall, required perfect aim and timing from the crew. "The team play of the open hearth," one worker recalled, was "like a house-raising in the community." It "was not a beginner's job. You must swing your weapon through a wide arc, to give it 'wing' and stuff must hop off just behind the furnace door and rise high enough to top the scrap between and land high."

## PUT TO THE TEST

Open hearth workers continually tested the composition of the melted charge. "Taking the test" was hot and dangerous. By 1946, when this photo was taken, samples extracted from the furnace were sent by pneumatic tubes to laboratories for analysis.

Previously the testing had been completed right on the spot, as crews broke open samples to see if the right grade of steel had been achieved.

## INFERNO

Workers hurried to safety as roaring sirens warned that the "heat" was ready to be poured at Stelco in 1940. Seconds later, a dynamite charge tore a hole in the back of the furnace wall. A torrent of molten steel burst into the ladle, throwing off showers of sparks and dense clouds of smoke.

## TEEMING INGOTS

This Dominion Foundries crew was "teeming the heat," directing molten steel from a ladle into waiting ingot moulds, during the 1930s. Cooled ingots were stripped from the moulds and rolled into desired lengths and thicknesses in a finishing mill.

Workers wore no faceguards or safety suits while they "teemed the heat," and stood completely exposed to flying sparks and small explosions of red-hot steel.

## THROUGH THE MILL

A crew of "rollers" guided a heated bar into the rolling mill at Stelco's "Ontario Works" in 1942. The Ontario Works dated back to the 1860s when the Great Western Railway established a mill to reroll its iron rails. When Stelco was formed, the mill became part of the operations, and again serviced the railways by producing tie plates and splice bars.

Despite layoffs and transfers during the Depression, "rollers" remained a close-knit group of workers. Recalling fondly the teamwork that was essential among rollers, one 44-year veteran remembered that "It was always good to return to the old job."

## SHEET MILL MEN

Sheet metal crews were a notorious lot who worked hard and played hard. They stuck together, and they brooked no interference with their independence on the job.

In 1936, Stelco managers placed a "safety donkey" in the mill as a penalty to shame the men into achieving a better safety record. The donkey was destroyed and this poem was penned:

*There is many an attempt to bring workers to contempt*
  *And employers often seem to "play the fool"*
*There is many an example but consider just one sample*
  *It's the homely hundred dollar Stelco mule.*

*The idea, so I gather, is that workingmen would rather*
  *Get injured and reduce their scanty wage;*
*But departments will abhor having donkey at their door,*
  *So reduce or wipe lost time from off their page.*

*But more subtle is the reason for both in and out of season,*
  *Costs are cut and all the cuts come from our pay,*
*If the Donkey we debate, then our wage increase must wait,*
  *Till it's "Come across, or else...," is what we say.*

*But the Donkey, it is stated, once was really decorated,*
  *When he went to the department making sheets,*
*On his sign so span and spik, we were warned about his kick*
  *What it later said, the editor deletes.*

*At an early morning hour he was found beneath a shower,*
  *When his owner sent and rescued him from there,*
*His doom was just as near, for a fire attacked his rear*
  *And he had to leave the damage to repair.*

*Now the moral, may I mention, is All Workers Pay Attention,*
  *Do not speed up to become the Company's fool!*
*From your wages keep their chisel and this racket soon will fizzle*
  *Then there won't be any kick in Stelco's mule.*

## COREMAKERS

Workers flanked a core they had prepared for use in one of Dominion Foundries' mammoth castings around 1930.

A core was a lump of specially treated sand, often with a molasses adhesive, which was shaped, baked hard, and placed in a mould.

During a pour, metal flowed into the mould and around the core. The mould gave a casting its external shape. The core, once removed from the hardened metal, gave the casting its internal space.

## MANPOWER

Every muscle strained as these moulders guided a hundred-pound pour of molten iron at International Harvester in the 1940s.

Walter King tried to take up the trade during the 1930s. "Well," he recalls, "at that time I weighed 140 pounds. A ladle was pretty near as heavy as I was, so that was just out of the question. I could carry a ladle of iron but I couldn't run with it. And I couldn't carry it too far. You've got to get it under your leg and run with it without spilling it. It's heavy! I wasn't strong enough."

## STANDING BY

This "bottom pour" at Dominion Foundries in the late 1920s required the co-operation of an entire department. Overhead cranes delivered the enormous ladles of bubbling steel from large electric furnaces to the men who waited to guide the pour into the giant mould.

The complex and delicate operation demanded judgements which defied mere text-book knowledge and could only be made after years of on-the-job experience. Thus, the pouring of large castings drew the critical eye of many a foundryman who had participated in some aspect of the moulding.

## A GRIND

Straddling a casting in the chipping department, this man ground away sand and roughness from the surface of the steel at Dominion Foundries in the 1920s.

So much sand and noise filled the air that one veteran "chipper" named it the hazard area. "We inhaled the silica sand and that's how I got silicosis. Compared with another shop such as the plate mill, tin mill and machine shop, the chip shop was the worst, the hardest job."

## FORGING VICTORY

"Wars make steel companies," long-time Stelco employee Johnny Shipperbottom recalled. "The First Great War made the Steel Company. The Second Great War made Dofasco."

This crew forged an anti-aircraft barrel at Dofasco during World War II. War orders brought peak production to Hamilton's steel industry. The slack employment of the Depression era gave way to gruelling ten and eleven hour days, seven days a week. From 1939 to 1946, output per worker increased more than two and a half times.

## PAY DAY

Workers lined up to be paid by number at Dominion Foundries during the 1930s.

Although steel was considered a high-wage industry, most steelworkers' families lived below the poverty line. Even in 1946, unionized steelworkers fell short of winning pay increases that would have brought labourers' wages in line with standards which the Toronto Welfare Council defined as "minimum decency" for a family of five.

CHECK
Number
1500
To
5100

# WOMEN WORKERS

A moulder's wife fetched wood for the family kitchen in 1910.

# Bring Your Sisters

The woman pictured on the opposite page gathered kindling for her kitchen stove in 1910, much as women had done centuries before. Time stood still in household technology, a striking contrast with the ever-changing industrial world. House-wives, after all, worked for no pay. They produced no profit for any employer. As a result, there was no pressure to mechanize housework and cut labour costs.

Women's role in the household economy cast a long shadow over every aspect of their participation in the wage economy. It determined the age of the female workforce labouring for wages. Housework was a fulltime job which confined almost all married women to the home. Thus, women wage workers were invariably young and single, quite literally "working girls."

The low economic value placed on housework also affected the wages of domestics and housekeepers, the most common of female occupations until 1914. In 1935, a "sympathizer" wrote to the *Spectator* about the typical case of a live-in domestic paid eight dollars a month in return for five hours work per day: "five hours per day, no starting or finishing time, all the housework including waxing and polishing the floors, assist with the cooking... all washing and laundry... and care of the child while the parents are away... Five hours per day, 30 days per month, 150 hours per month works out to exactly five and one-third cents per hour."

The stereotypes about women's "primary" responsibilities also allowed employers to justify discriminatory practices that were never tolerated among men. From the beginning, employers restricted women to a select range of labour-intensive occupations such as food processing, light manufacturing and secretarial work — what is now called the female job ghetto. All of these jobs demanded patience and dexterity. All were closely supervised, usually by men. All were poorly paid.

On an average, women earned a full 40 percent less than men. Some critics blamed the women themselves for passively accepting these low wages, as if wage levels were a matter of choice. But women did not choose their wages. Their wages were determined by the forces of prejudice and power. Since all women entered the workforce with a similar range of household-related skills that they had learned as children, their skill-level was underrated. Their work, like housework itself, was undervalued, regarded at best as "nimble." Their wages fell to the lowest level of the unskilled. Since all women were forced to compete for a narrow range of jobs, the female labour market was chronically oversupplied. Wages fell to the lowest level of subsistence.

Even professionally-trained women were segregated in certain lines of work commonly referred to as the "helping professions." Women nurses, teachers and social workers were expected to display the maternal virtues of self-sacrifice, sensitivity and warmth. They were not respected for the leadership, independent judgement and salaries that went with professionalism.

Despite these problems, working women were neither passive nor depressed. Most looked back on their working years as a positive experience and recalled the independence and good times they enjoyed. Childhood had often been spent alone at home, helping mother with household chores. The years at work offered comparative freedom and time for socializing with friends. As a result, working women jealously defended their right to enjoy themselves on their own free time. Many snubbed their noses at paternalistic do-gooders who were ever fretful that good times led to sin. One "working girl" wrote to the Hamilton *Herald* in 1913 and denounced the hypocrisy of "several gentlemen" who had lashed out at the supposed lax morality of women workers. "Working girl" insisted that "all work and no play makes Jack a dull boy. Instead of some of the employers of the city interesting themselves in the 'white slave' traffic, and girls going astray, if they would look into the pay envelopes of their employees on pay day, they might see how such evils exist. Girls, after all, are only human, and naturally want to share in the good things of life as much as their luckier sisters."

World War II provided a brief exception to the standard treatment of working women. Face to face with a severe "manpower" shortage, employers turned to women as a "reserve" of labour and opened the doors to a variety of heavy industrial jobs, including skilled ones. Governments subsidized day care centres which freed married women to enter the labour force. Women of all ages seized the opportunity to work at new jobs. Once the war was over, however, governments closed down the daycare centres, and industrial employers laid off their women workers. As far as governments and employers were concerned, women belonged back with church, children and kitchen.

## MARKET DAY

Housewives haggled over prices and quality, feigning indifference to the appeals of a huckster carting his wares around the James Street Market in 1908. Market shoppers had to be aggressive but discriminating as they "bustled and scurried, crowded each other good naturedly, pinched fruit indiscriminately, tasted butter timidly, and in the end, made their heavily laden way homeward, tired and worn-out, but satisfied," according to a contemporary *Spectator* report.

## WASH DAY

This houswife jingled some clothespegs in her pocket before hanging her hand-washed laundry out on the clothesline to dry. She scanned the vegetable garden, chicken coops, and rabbit hutches she had to tend when the laundry was dried and ironed. In the evening, she helped put the finishing touches to the additions her husband was continually making to their suburban home on Hamilton Mountain. Most settlers on Hamilton Mountain during the 1920s built their homes a little at a time, as money became available. Savings could not be diverted to labour-saving home appliances. Only with the rise of credit buying in the 1950s did such appliances as clothes dryers and automatic washers become more available to working class households.

Canada's pioneer heritage remained a fact of life for Canadian housewives long after the backwoods era of roughing it in the bush. Mechanization, specialization and concentration of labour advanced at a snail's pace in the household economy, lagging far behind the transformations taking place in the paid labour market. Housework was the last occupation to be "modernized." It was a full-time job which kept almost all married women out of the paid workforce until the 1950s.

## GIRLFRIENDS

These Bell Telephone operators and friend sported daring bathing suits for a week of unchaperoned holiday frolic in 1914. Working girls were often criticized for such outlandish behaviour.

Young women workers rejoiced in the relative freedom and independence of their working years, which they often contrasted to the drudgery, isolation and discipline of childhood years spent helping in the home. Unlike boys, most of whom enjoyed a relatively permissive and freewheeling childhood, working girls looked upon their adolescent years on the job market in terms of free time off the job, a brief fling sandwiched in between long stretches of past and future household responsibilities. Decades later, those interviewed still savoured memories of close friendships and fun-filled evenings, almost to the exclusion of actual workplace experiences.

Since working girls cherished their independence, they resented paternalistic employers who assumed the authority of parents and fretted about the supposed low morality rather than the low wages of their employees.

## THE SMELL OF FINE TOBACCO

A male taskmaster frowned forbiddingly down the long tables where women workers sifted through stacks of leaves for use in blended cigarette tobacco.

One woman who worked at Tuckett's during the early 1930s, some 20 years after this photograph was taken, remembered that ventilation was virtually non-existent. "I hated the smell of tobacco. It used to make me sick. I think it made everybody sick. But the pay was all right, so we didn't worry too much about the smell."

On hot summer days, she recounted, "people used to faint, especially the Italian ladies. Some of them were pretty well built and it would be too much for them, especially when the wind came a certain way, and that burley tobacco would just hit you."

## PACKING IT IN

Women workers kept their eyes fixed downward as they clenched an olive with one hand and delivered three quick flicks of the knife with the other. One motion plucked out the pit, the next wedged in a slice of pimento, the third lodged the olive inside the bottle so that the pimento faced outward. One male supervised the table of women repeating this job at McLaren's food processing plant during the 1920s.

The Hamilton-area foodpacking industry boomed in the early 1900s and drew in hundreds of women. In 1906 a provincial medical inspector found the working conditions "disgusting," but by the 1920s public criticism resulted in higher sanitary standards, at least for the workers. The caps and gowns worn by McLaren workers were thought to prevent human germs from contaminating the food.

## SEWN UP

A seamstress towelled off the sweat from her forehead, draped the towel over her shoulder and stretched her legs. Once the picture was taken, she swivelled back into her chair, started pumping on the footpedal that powered her sewing machine, and tugged a stuffed mattress along for its final seam.

The photograph was taken in the 1920s at the Membery Mattress Company, a small factory on the fringes of the sewing industry. Women increasingly replaced male tailors in the needle trades once standardized mass production techniques developed in the ready-made clothing industry.

## COTTON PICKIN'

Specks of cotton swirled around this worker at the Canadian Cottons plant in the 1940s, as she watched over machinery that cleaned and straightened the raw cotton fibres into the loose ropes, or "sliver," filling the cans on the right. Later in the production process, the sliver would be "drawn" into finer strands and then spun, to be ready for weaving into cloth.

Women filled a large number of the machine-tending jobs in the three Hamilton plants which produced cotton cloth. It was not healthy work. As the picture reveals, the air was full of fibres that theatened workers with "brown lung" disease.

## SNIPPING AWAY

Under the watchful eye of the foreman, these cutters at Mercury Mills in 1928 snipped the knitted cloth into the necessary shapes for sweaters or sportswear.

A woman who worked in a knitting mill during the 1930s can still point to a kink in one finger. "That's from holding the scissors all the time," she explains. After standing on hard floors day after day, many women in jobs like these also suffered from stiff joints or varicose veins.

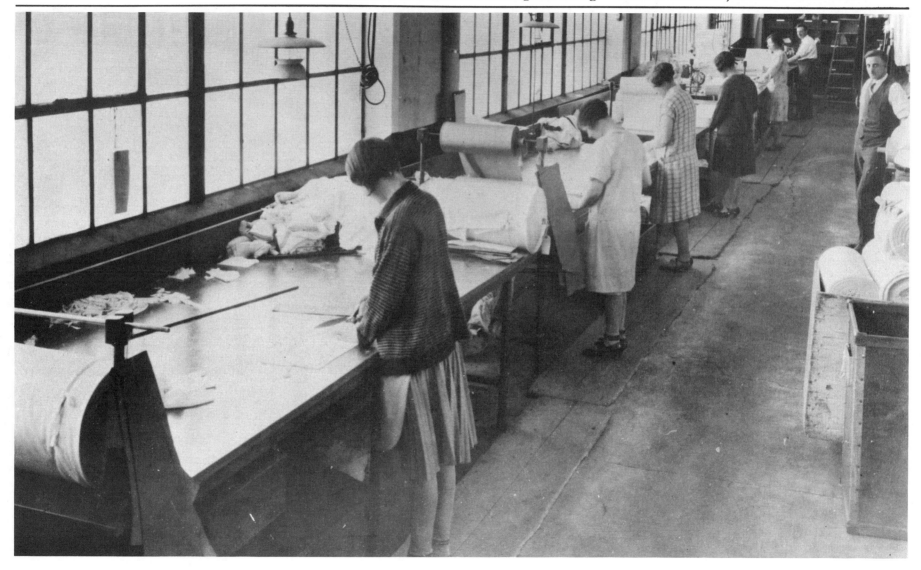

## TIME AND MOTION

Women assembled radio parts at Westinghouse in 1947 while a supervisor looked over their shoulders, marking their time in his notebook.

Despite the painstaking care required in these jobs — some parts weighed as little as 1/700th of an ounce — women rarely enjoyed workplace independence or control over the pace of production. Unlike artisanal craftsmen who commonly exercised this autonomy, women were subjected to highly regimented task systems and "speed up" schemes which monitored their every time and motion.

Madge Greig worked at Westinghouse during the 1930s and recalled: "My father always told me that 'in this country it's the speed that counts.' And right enough, in the Westinghouse you'd have the timer standing right over your shoulder. You'd make your time for a while, then the first thing you know, he's back again and you had to do better. Better and better. It was like that all the time."

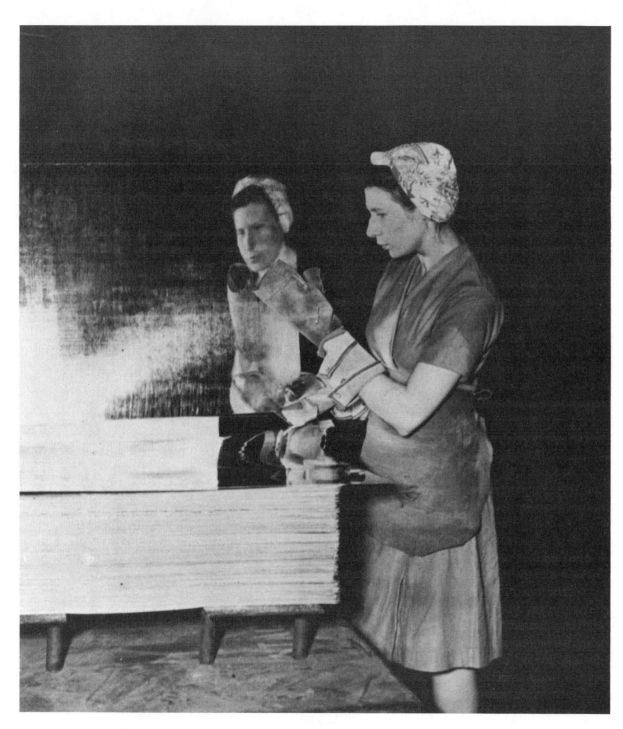

## TINFLIPPER

A tinflipper inspected both sides of a tin plate for imperfections at Stelco in 1947. These women "either got very strong, or they got tendonitis," a Dofasco executive commented.

Tinflipping was one of the few jobs open to women in steel mills across North America. Industry folklore held that men quickly became bored and careless at the job. Women were preferred because of their reputation for quick hands and patient eyes, traits that were supposedly inherited after countless centuries of knitting and sewing. These stereotyped qualities did not win women rights to other jobs in the industry.

## WOUND UP

Westinghouse women were "wizards at winding," the company's Hamilton employee magazine declared in 1946.

The paper reported that 220 employees "mostly quick-fingered girls, are entrusted with the manufacture of Westinghouse coils." Coil winding was considered "an interesting occupation calling for skill and application. Foremen add that patience is another necessary qualification for this important work.... In a year 32,240,000 feet of wire is used for transformer distribution coils alone."

The women pictured in this 1947 photograph wound refrigerator motors.

## MA BELL'S DAUGHTERS

In 1891, women telephone operators worked the boards under the eyes of a male overseer who barked out instructions through a primitive microphone. By 1948, women operators worked the boards under the eyes of a female overseer who could overhear and instruct each operator individually. The operating staff had been entirely female since 1890. Earlier experiments using young boys proved a failure when the quick-tempered lads insulted complaining customers.

Although Bell's job descriptions idealized the operator's job as white collar work, the company's strict supervision of fast-paced and nerve-wracking mechanical operations was patterned directly after the factory.

## WHITE COLLAR

Women clerical workers typed, filed and took dictation at the B. Greening Wire office in the early 1900s. At that time, women were just beginning to make their way into the male world of errand boys, man-fridays and clerks on their way up the managerial ladder. By 1944, when this Sawyer Massey secretary swivelled between typewriter and switchboard, office work was a "traditional" field of women's employment.

As the white collar sector expanded afer 1900 in response to the planning needs of far-flung corporate empires, office work became increasingly mechanized and routine.

A stylized description of the Westinghouse Transcribing Department in 1943 gave an indication of the role and skill of these workers. "Nineteen girls wearing earphones sit at electrically operated typwriters. Hearing what you and 89 other correspondents in twelve departments have to say, their dancing fingers convey the messages accurately to paper. In a single month these girls handle 14,000 letters, orders and miscellaneous typing assignments..."

Despite their training, manual dexterity and responsibility, typists and secretaries rarely approached half the salary level of occupations such as printing. Typesetting was done by men; it was regarded as a skill. Typing was done by women; it was regarded as nimble and semi-skilled.

## SCHOOLDAYS

Students at Hamilton's teachers' college learned how to teach sewing in 1909. Almost all public school teachers were women. Even though males were paid twice as much as similarly qualified females, the salary level was still too low to attract men.

Home economics (domestic science) was a new field of study at this time. Adelaide Hoodless, wife of a Hamilton manufacturer and a leading figure in the National Council of Women and Women's Institute, pioneered the home economics movement as a means of preparing schoolgirls "for their God-given place in life" as mothers. Hoodless believed that this training also prepared a girl to be "conscious of her duty to her employer and herself" during her few "transitional years" in the workforce. The school system did not, however, send women into the workforce with any training in industrial skills.

Ontario's Inspector of Technical Education reported, in 1909, that "In all discussions of the Trade and Technical School question it is to be regretted that the treatment of this matter generally centres round the man, and the woman's side of it is very largely neglected... Industrial training for men has many friends and few enemies, but while industrial training for women as far as it is applied to the home is looked upon with favour, any special training to place girls in skilled trades has many enemies and few friends."

## BABIES AND BEDPANS

Nurses instructed immigrants on Canadian methods of child-rearing at the Hamilton Health Centre baby clinic during the 1920s.

Concern for public health, cleanliness and post-medical aftercare elevated nursing duties and training to a para-professional level during the 1890s. Prior to that, Hamilton nurses were kept busy with such menial jobs as changing the straw in the mattresses of a hospital's "public ward." One patient asked for a change of nurses because the assigned one was "not strong enough to do our big family washing."

By 1900, nursing was regarded as a "helping profession." It was considered the ideal "womanly profession," one which respected male dominance in the medical world while striving after sensitivity and self-sacrificing community service (for low pay) in the female world.

The public health area also challenged one of Hamilton's first women doctors, Elizabeth Bagshaw. When she arrived in Hamilton in 1906, smallpox, typhoid, polio, influenza and even malaria epidemics caused yearly panics. She was one of the first doctors to promote smallpox vaccination in the city.

In her years of practice, Dr. Bagshaw saw countless mothers who lived in fear of having their health and shaky family finances undermined by additional children. Although it was illegal to distribute birth control information or devices, Dr. Bagshaw took charge of the Hamilton Birth Control Society during the 1930s. "We did it quietly," she recalled, "but the Catholic Bishop did object and he would speak out against the birth control clinic at public meetings.... The next week, we'd have double the number of women at the clinic. He gave us the best publicity we ever had."

## BRING YOUR SISTERS TOO

"Canadian Women Assume Arduous Tasks Making Steel to Allow their Menfolk to Join Colours to Fight Huns."

Thus *Stelco Flashes* reported on one of the most important developments of the World War II period, the opening of heavy industrial work to women of all ages. "A wide variety of jobs, hitherto regarded as strictly outside the abilities of the so-called weaker sex are now being performed at Stelco, in extremely capable fashion by Mrs. and Miss Janie Canuck," the paper reported. "Keep it up, girls, and bring more of your sisters along too." The young "sisters" who came to Stelco included Mina Mitchell, who began working at Stelco at the age of 12 in 1942.

## ROSIE THE RIVETER

Women workers at National Steel Car ate lunch, socialized and organized a pool at the company cafeteria in 1944.

"Rosie the Riveter" could well have been a Canadian, according to this description in the February, 1944 issue of National Steel Car's company magazine, *The Car Builder*.

"Cranes rumble overhead, horns blare as they carry their heavy loads. The whirring whine of the reamers is mocked by the hissing spit of the welding torches. The bull riveters snort defiantly and the open gas furnaces roar their blazing anger. There is the rasping sound of the grinders, sending a myriad of sparks dancing through the air, and the ring of steel on steel.

"Above these and many other clashing sounds is the pounding chatter of dozens of rivet guns driving at once. While this strange symphony clamours about them the ladies of Steel Erection work with casual confidence and caution.

"Mary Morrison is a heater. Tongs in her right hand, her left on the handle of the heater, Mary places three cold black rivets in the copper jaws of her machine. In a moment they are white hot. Her foot presses down one of the pedals at the base of her machine, tongs grip the rivet firmly, she draws it out and flips her wrist. It has no sooner left her tongs than she has another in its place.

"Plank! A trail of sparks tracing its path through the air, her 'sticker' Mary Ostrowski catches it expertly in her 'catch can'. She fishes it out with her pick-ups and 'sticks' it. The bucker holds it in place with his bucking bar and the riveter's hammer chatters.

## TRADESWOMEN

The "manpower" shortage was so severe that some women gained the chance to learn a skilled trade.

National Steel Car began training women welders in 1941 and reported that "they are surprising the experts and the old hands by their ability to take a man's place on a vital home front job... And to top it off, when they raise their welding hoods for a minute or two, it does brighten up the shop to see a smiling young lass!"

## PICK AND SHOVEL

"The plant could never have survived without them," claimed one Stelco manager who witnessed scenes such as this one in 1940. "Three of them would lift those very heavy rails, carry it to its proper position, and lay it down. They could use a sledge hammer better than a lot of men I've seen."

The women realized their own importance and refused to put up with harassment. One woman told a leering foreman "where to go and then threatened to hit him on the backside with the g-- d-- shovel if he didn't stop," a co-worker recalled fondly.

## FROM FAR AND WIDE

Audrey Ainsworth operated a small coil winder at Westinghouse in 1945. In one department, 360,000 coils were wound for bomb racks alone.

To meet their staffing needs, companies such as Westinghouse sent recruiting agents into the Canadian north and west. That is how Vida Richards of Dundurn, Saskatchewan, came to Westinghouse in 1943. Fed up with low-paying domestic and restaurant work, she sought out and enthusiastically completed a government course in machine work. Then she was brought East. At Westinghouse, she noticed, "most of the women enjoyed it thoroughly — it was a nice change from cleaning up."

Mrs. Richards also recalled the independence that was typical of war workers. A fur-coated lady once approached her group of friends and condescended to roll down her car window to ask if she could assist them. "We look after ourselves," was the unanimous reply. They then proceeded to the dance-hall, where they danced with one another, young men being in short supply during the war.

"During the war," former Westinghouse local union president Alf Ready remembered, "women came from all over, many from the west. I would say that the girls who came from the west and had a Ukrainian background were really solid (unionists). Generally, the women were not as pro-union as the men. But those who were, were right in there. At least two women were on the executive..."

## COME ON CANADA

"Women! Back Them Up — To Bring Them Back." This and other government slogans urged women war workers, such as this Sawyer Massey machinist in 1943, to "man" the production front out of patriotic duty.

A typical pen-portrait in the 1942 *Car Builder* referred to 16 year old Linda, who "doesn't remember much about Estonia. But she grits pretty teeth at the thought of the Huns who have enslaved her homeland. You see, her grandmother, uncles, aunts and cousins are still in the old country. Maybe that's one reason why Linda bought a Victory Bond during the recent campaign.

"...Boy friends? The one and only is in the R.C.A.F. at Brantford training to be a pilot officer. Some day he may drop a bomb for Linda on the Germans in Estonia."

Despite the deluge of propaganda, many women had their own ideas. "Before the war came, I thought I would spend the rest of my life on the farm," recalled one. "But when the war came, I saw the chance for a little independence." Another remembered that "I wanted to work at Stelco because it meant I could live on my own in a city and I could afford to have some fun before I got married."

## DAY CARE

A 1942 government study of the *Reserve of Labour Among Canadian Women* noted that married women between 15 and 40 were "a labour pool practically untapped." The next year, government subsidized day care was made available to mothers working in war industries.

"It must indeed be difficult for mothers to relinquish the care of their children to someone else," the woman's columnist for the National Steel Car's magazine *The Car Builder* imagined, "but today, with such a big job to be done, they feel they can bring husbands home sooner by pitching in and helping. These mothers, I'm sure, must be able to work more wholeheartedly, knowing their sons and daughters are safe and well-cared for."

Government-assisted daycare was launched in Hamilton in 1943. Hamilton's three centres offered care from 6:30 a.m. to 6:00 p.m. and provided children with two meals and a snack. Nursery teacher Raye Lebow, standing here with children in 1944, took pride in the quality care that was offered. A trained staff of four supervised a maximum of 40 children. Most children gained five to seven pounds within a year of attendance. The fee was 50 cents a day for children of two working parents, 35 cents a day for children of single parents.

Hamilton's three centres were closed after the war, despite the protests of nursery staff, when local and provincial governments refused to provide further subsidies. The reserve of labour among Canadian women would henceforth be tapped without government and company measures to provide back-up services or equal training opportunities for women. The war for democracy was over.

# RECREATION

Stylishly-hatted Westinghouse workers headed home, around 1910.

# The Times We Used to Have

Before 1946, Hamilton workers never knew what it was like to sigh "Thank God it's Friday." After working five ten-hour days, they still had a five-hour shift to put in on Saturday morning. But as Saturday noon approached, the turn-of-the-century Hamilton poet and newspaper columnist R.K. Kernighan tells us,

*A thrill runs through the worker's breast.*
*And they who labor for their bread*
*Will give their weary hearts a rest.*

*Ten thousand eats will hark to hear*
*The joyous whistles shriek at noon;*
*For health and joy and peace are near*
*A blessing and a boon.*

*The girls will don their dresses white*
*And with the lads from toil immune*
*Will joyous be from noon to night —*
*Sweet Saturday afternoon.*

By the standards of today, early styles of recreation seem simple and uncomplicated, perhaps even dull and tiresome. Adults fixed up their homes, planted gardens and tended to rabbits and pigeons, all necessary activities if a family was to have adequate food on a workingman's wages. Children had few toys, but made their own fun on streets, vacant lots and waterfronts. "We had a lot of fun just looking around," one woman who grew up in the 1930s recalled. "We had very little so we were happy with what we had. We didn't know any different, and, you know, I wouldn't trade that time for all the money in the world."

Paid vacations were unheard of for blue collar workers. Even on holidays such as Christmas and Easter, many workers were simply laid off for the day. Thus, workers had to take full advantage of the city's immediate natural and social setting. Families went on outings to Burlington Beach or took the old Incline Railway to the woods on Hamilton Mountain. They passed time with their workmates and neighbours, most of whom lived in tightly-knit, often ethnically-based, comunities.

Of course, Hamilton has always been a city of avid sports fans. Star athletes made local teams like the Tigers, Wildcats and Alerts nationally famous. Fans were not content just to cheer on the plays of others. Scores of amateur teams, often linked directly to workplaces, unions and political clubs, bred a spirit of activism, solidarity and social awareness. In the early 1930s, an awestruck lad edged up to members of Hamilton Mountain's all-star ball team to ask about the name emblazoned on their T-shirts — Marxian Youth. That's how Harold Keeton, later a prominent official with the United Rubber Workers at Firestone, first came into contact with radical politics.

There were more serious pursuits as well. Workingmen led the agitation which resulted in the city's first public library in the 1890s. Later, workers launched organizations for their own self-improvement, such as the East Hamilton Progressive Association or the Workers' Educational Association. Many spent their evenings upgrading their trade skills at the new technical school.

By the turn of the century, a rash of laws forbade almost every form of energetic recreation on Sundays. This rigid Sabbath observance must have seemed hypocritical to steelworkers, street railwaymen and deliverymen who were required to work on Sundays. There were stern rules for the rest of the week as well. All the new dance crazes were denounced by local clergymen. Dancing the tango cost one telephone operator her job in 1914. The same year, in the midst of a depression, the police commission denounced movie theatres. They "might create a tendency to spend too much money," the police worried. Prohibitionists had long tried to wean the

workingman from his glass of beer. During World War I, they succeeded in banning the bar and bringing an end to the camaraderie of the local tavern. These "social purity" enthusiasts continued to press their grim moralism during the depression of the 1930s. They campaigned to close newly re-opened beverage rooms at 10 in the evening, to suppress dance halls, bingo and "housie housie" games.

When employers learned that they could not stop workingmen from joining in active recreation, they decided to beat them at their own games. Many corporations tried to harness their workers' favourite pastimes to promote a sense of community inside the plant and a spirit of loyalty to the firm. By the 1920s, company-sponsored leagues were a permanent fixture in the recreational life of the community.

At the same time, the "entertainment industry" was born. "Creeping commercialism" began to change older patterns of spontaneous and locally-based recreation. After a long day's work, many people liked to escape to the tinselled world of vaudeville and movie houses, to share a laugh at a Charlie Chaplin comedy or shed a tear at a Mary Pickford romance. Thousands flocked into stadiums to watch the new professional athletes. This

packaged entertainment sapped some of the creativity out of recreation.

Finally, the space for informal recreation in the city shrank considerably. Vacant lots and even a few parks disappeared as the city grew and spread. The waterfront became an exclusive landscape for industry as companies hoarded all available space and spewed their untreated pollution into the bay.

In the early 1900s, men shot ducks along the shores of Hamilton Bay. Boys spent their lunch hours catching fish. The new Hamilton — dirtier and more congested — destroyed this easy, casual rapport with nature. After World War II, people had to travel far from home to find the same pleasures.

None of these developments suppressed the ingenuity of Hamilton's working people in their efforts to enjoy the pleasures of life. There was no single style of working class leisure. Some whiled away their time in streets and taverns. Some were homebodies. Some burnt the midnight oil trying to improve their education. There was variety as well as vitality in the ways working people used their precious hours off the job. It revealed the independence and resourcefulness that lay untapped in The Ambitious City.

## FAMILY PORTRAIT

May 24, 1886, was the wedding day for this Hamilton widower and his bride, herself a widowed cousin of the groom's first wife. Before marrying, Benjamin Fowler had been forced to give up his moulder's job at Burrow, Stewart, and Milne foundry so that he could take proper care of his four children.

Savings from his previous work and odd jobs in the community kept the family financially solvent. For one job, he carried his youngest child on his arm while climbing the belfry ladder at Ascension Church to ring the bells for a dollar a week.

Respectability was maintained throughout all these difficulties. A correct correspondence with his wife's cousin brought her to Hamilton. On the wedding day, a splendid false back-drop was properly in place during the required visit to a photographer's studio. The whole family then rode to visit the children's grandmother in Dundas. After raising his family alone for a year and a half, he returned to foundry work. Fowler died from cancer in 1907.

Against all odds, workers still aspired to a respectable lifestyle. In 1907, the *Industrial Banner* discussed "what the workingman wants" for himself and his family.

"He wants shorter hours that he may enjoy the society of his wife and children. He wants to take a holiday from his labor every year. He wants his family to dress well and live on the best. He wants his girls to take music lessons and his boys to graduate from high school and the knowledge that he can live well, enjoy life and put a little money in the bank every week. He sees no just reason why a man who does nothing can squander twenty thousand dollars on a game of cards while an industrious mechanic cannot earn that amount of wages in as many years. In other words, the twentieth century workingman wants more of the good things in life. He wants life to be worth living."

85

## THEIR OWN HOME

Relatives and neighbours pitched in to help this Italian family build their own house during the 1920s. Families skimped and saved to build their homes in a pre-credit version of the installment plan: each new addition was installed when savings and time became available.

A 1913 government report on the cost of living accused these homebuilders of false economy and pride, which "induces families to live in the best possible houses and neighbourhoods at the expense of needs wherein economies can be made less obtrusive, as for instance in diet." The *Labor News* countered that home ownership was the only way to escape "the clutches of some of the city's avaricious landlord shylocks." In sacrificing their time, money and health, homebuilders helped Hamilton avoid the fate of a tenement city.

## OUT THE BACK

Loungers had standing room only in back yards cramped with clothes lines, vegetable gardens and work spaces. These women took advantage of a sunny day in the 1940s to prepare tomato paste in the fresh air of downtown Hamilton.

In 1910, promoters of the new Brightside subdivision in the east-end advertised the "fine quality of the soil. It is suitable for growing vegetables and is itself a big consideration for the thrifty workman, as he may live on a comparatively small piece of ground... raise his year's supply of staple vegetables without much trouble and less expense." Brightside became the heart of the Italian community in Hamilton.

## DEMON RUM

The era of bootleg liquor staggered to a halt by the late 1920s, but this old fellow couldn't give up a decade-long habit of taking his snort on the sly.

Many workingmen looked forward to a glass of ale at the end of the working day. A man who unloaded coal on the Hamilton waterfront in the early 1900s recalled that the crew regularly "went over to Gompf's Brewery for a keg of beer to wash the dust from their insides."

Middle class reformers, employers and a good number of working class teetotalers wanted to ban the bar, which they saw as destructive of industrial discipline and healthy home life. In 1916, prohibitionists convinced the provincial government to outlaw the sale of alcohol.

Many workers were outraged, and some Hamiltonians joined a 5,000-man march on Queen's Park in 1918 to demand the return of strong beer. But to no avail. Taverns were shut down for more than a decade.

Radio succeeded where prohibitionists failed. It brought families together and centred recreation in the home, thereby helping to stamp out the "idle" male culture centred in streets and bars. By the 1940s, families spent their evenings at home, huddled around the radio to catch the latest in music, sports, stories and news of the war.

Unlike the local story-tellers, neighbourhood get-togethers and public forums that it replaced, radio was a one-way medium. It offered no face-to-face contact or dialogue.

## ON THE BEACH

This family escaped the swelter of a factory town and cooled off — as much as bathing fashions would permit — in the clear waters of Hamilton Bay.

Working class families could not afford the drive to cottage country, but Hamilton Bay and Burlington Beach offered a pleasant alternative for fishermen, beachcombers and swimmers alike. "The water in Hamilton Bay was so clear," one old-timer remarked, "that you could see Rocco Perri," a local bootlegger who mysteriously disappeared in the 1940s.

## DOWN HILL

A group of tobogganers paused for a photographer before taking the great leap downward on Hamilton Mountain in the 1890s.

One North Ender recalled the makeshift style of entertainment that flourished when open spaces were still close to the heart of the city.

"There was a great bobsled run on Mary Street that ran about four blocks right down to Ferrie Street. There were no cars then, remember, only horses. The people used to get out there at night, with great big washtubs full of water, and flood the hill. Holy Hannah, twelve o'clock at night, they would finish flooding the hill and come down — some of those bobsleds would hold ten or twelve people. They had four blocks to walk back, but they would go."

## SUMMERTIME
A gang of North End kids basked in the attention of two local artists in the 1930s. Printmaker and photographer Leonard Hutchinson captured the little rascals as they pranced back and forth to monitor the progress of a sketching painter.

## LABOUR IN CONCERT

Workers had the brass to form up in parade for Hamilton's centennial celebrations in 1913.

It was a nice break for the band, which usually practised on the muddy terrain of a new working class suburb in the East End. The band was an adjunct of the East Hamilton Progressive Association, a workingman's club formed in 1912.

"The new society will not be an organization merely to look after the material wants of the members of the district," announced the *Herald*, "but will also engage in educational work. It is proposed that it will conduct debates at almost every meeting, when questions such as municipal ownership, single tax, licensing laws, social evils, arbitration as used in labor issues, etc., will be debated. The society has adopted the model Principia Non Homines (principles, not men), and will adhere strictly to this motto."

## OFF THE DIAMOND

This sandlot team of street railwaymen included some jokers and some deadly-earnest ball players.

Their lively informal style was not always appreciated. "A resident of South MacNab street called at the police office this afternoon," the *Herald* reported in 1910, "to complain about the employees of the factories in that district playing ball during the dinner hour on the street."

Thirty-five years later, a retired Greening wire weaver recalled his workmates' boundless energy in pick-up sports and decried the passing of close relations on and off the job. "You were on the same bench all day and on the same baseball field in the evening. Things are different now. Things move more quickly; men are busier. You don't see one another from the time the shop closes until it opens up next day. I miss the times we used to have."

**PERMIT TO LEAVE CANADA**

9921

(Schedule B. to Order in Council of May 24, 1917)

I, *Martin Wilk*

of *794 Burlington East Hamilton*
(If town or city give street address).

in the Province of *Ontario*, make oath and do

say that I was born at *Chenstochof Russia* on the *9th*

day of *November*, 18*73*, that I am a (an)

*Russian* (subject) (citizen) by (birth)

(naturalization); that I have resided at the above address for *6 years in*
(Length of

*Hamilton* that I am personally known to and refer for identification to:—
residence).

*Rancieuntz Paul* of *393 Sherman Ave*

*Thaginol Davis* of *385 Sherman Ave*

*Chesma Vizente* of *794 Burlington*

*Emil Wasink* of *794 Burlington*

that I desire permission to leave Canada to go to *Buffalo to*

*167 Titus Str* for the purpose of *visiting*

*Andrei Mattrofsky*

that I expect to be absent from Canada for *100 days*
(Length of absence)

My height is *5/4*; my weight is *160*

My eyes are *brown*; my hair is *dark*

My occupation is *Laborer*

The attached photograph is a good likeness of

me taken *today* (months) (days) ago.

And I make this solemn declaration con-
scientiously believing it to be true and correct,
and knowing that it is of the same force and
effect as if made under oath and by virtue of
the Canada Evidence Act.

Declared before me at *Hamilton* in the

this *21st* day of *December* 19*17*

*Martin Wilk* *R. Sweeney*
Signature of Applicant.     Notary Public, J.P., Commissioner.

I have been personally acquainted with the above-mentioned applicant for

a period of ............................ (years) (months). I recognize the above attached

photo as a true likeness of him. I believe the statements which he makes above

to be correct and have seen him in my presence attach his signature on the same

line on which my own appears.

*Martin Wilk* *R. Sweeney*
Signature of Applicant.     Signature of Bank Manager, Chief of Police, Clergyman
                            or Dominion Government Officer.

*M. Wilk*

Canadian Immigration Inspector.

Permit to leave Canada on or before the ............ day of ............, 191...., is granted to

DEC 21 1917

"Any person to whom such written permission to leave Canada has been granted should carefully preserve the same and keep it always on his person.—See Sec. 1, Order-in-Council 1433."

## MOVING ON

Contrary to myths about stable communities in early Canada, most working people were constantly on the move. Immigrant workers had to criss-cross the continent in search of employment. Many stopped in Hamilton for only a brief stay before moving on. One Russian-born worker used this travel permit on his journeys.

Despite transiency, the so-called "foreign quarter" in Hamilton became a vibrant community with plenty of street life. "They live on the verandahs," the *Herald* reported in 1912, "and between forty and fifty have been known to sit on one. They are fond of the streets and are continually standing on them. The police had some difficulty in teaching them not to block the sidewalk..."

## MAJESTIC LUNCH

Before the days of fast-food outlets, small restaurants like the Majestic Lunch, shown here in the 1930s, often served as neighbourhood hangouts.

Max Boles recalls that in the Jewish quarter his family's delicatessen "was the meeting place for the older generation... They had no money, so spent the time playing pinochle and dominoes... Those characters would come home from peddling, maybe wash, eat and go directly to our store. This was five days a week...

"Many of our customers, as today, were afraid of their wives. When a belligerent wife would come in the front door, the husband would hop the fence in the rear and race for home."

## TEAMWORK

The new hair and dress styles of the 1920s were just beginning to show.

So were new styles of corporate management. Industrial relations experts urged companies to adopt sports and welfare programmes that could win workers to a better understanding of "industrial teamwork." As a result of these schemes, company-sponsored sports began to replace traditional patterns of informal and independently-organized recreation.

The days of the "Droops," a notoriously scruffy Westinghouse football squad that never won a game, were gone. Sprightly uniforms and formal leagues set the new tone, as evidenced in this Westinghouse women's softball team of 1920.

## CLOSER TOGETHER

Families stood in line to receive gifts for their children at a Dofasco Christmas party in the 1940s.

Dofasco had been playing Father Christmas to its employees since 1937 in an effort to strengthen the identity between workers' families and the family corporation. In 1938, the company's *Illustrated News* noted that everyone had a good time, especially the youngsters. "But let us look upon the friendly hour together in a different sense also. Did it bring us all closer together? If it did, it served its real purpose. It gave us an opportunity to mingle for a brief period with the wives and children and friends of our shopmates. We got to know them just a little more intimately."

## SWING YOUR PARTNER

Could square dancing help build unionism? Hamilton's steelworkers certainly thought so when they organized dances where unionists belted out the calls, not foremen.

Bill Scandlan, a Stelco steward during World War II, remembered, "There was a large number of girls... in the plant, and we... organized a little recreation in the Winter Gardens. We used to get a little band and we would charge a quarter and sell pop and so on and have a dance and everybody wanted to come to the dance. They had such a good time, and we wouldn't let them come unless they were a member of the union."

## COMPANY PICNIC

"We went to all the picnics," one Dofasco employee enthused. "To Galt and Port Dalhousie. We used to take the boat to Port Dalhousie. That was lots of fun! Every year! That was the big thing."

Dofasco introduced its annual company picnic during the 1930s and by 1943, when this picture was taken, it was a mass event.

The annual picnic was discontinued after the war. According to one management official, those employees left behind to maintain continuous operations resented workmates who got the day off. As well, the workforce became more self-reliant. Post-war workers had their own cars and government-legislated holidays, and were not so dependent on company patronage for a day's outing.

## EUCHRE!

A surprise play got a big laugh from lunchtime cardsharks working on street railway track in the 1940s. Good old-fashioned fun survived the toll of old-fashioned moralizing and new-fangled industrial relations schemes.

# PART II: A Union Town

# The Making of a Union Town

Hamilton is a city of two tales. It is a tale of ambition. Ambition is carved into Hamilton's very landscape, which was scooped and gouged by giant glaciers. It is written into its industrial landscape, which was churned and turned by huge foundries, mills and factories. It is written into its labour force, which was scraped and shaped by overpowering forces of technological and economic change.

Hamilton also has a tale of struggle, of unselfish ambition to improve the living standards, to raise the dignity and independence of its working people. Workers were not just controlled and victimized by the many changes that overtook the city. Through the labour movement, they became actors, not just bystanders, in their own history.

This history was created out of everyday life, not imported from outside or imposed by extraordinary individuals and groups. Sam Lawrence, the labour mayor of Hamilton during the epic strike wave of 1946, understood this. "The union program is not an impossible demand upon employers," he told a rally of strike supporters. "It has the down-to-earth reasonableness that day-to-day experience in the plants has given to our Hamilton workers."

This second section of the book builds on the everyday kinds of experiences we have documented thus far. This stucturing of the book parallels the processes of life itself. The labour movement was built out of the hardships which workers endured, the ingenuity and discipline which people practised at work, and the initiative and imagination which employers tried to deny.

As the following episodes of Hamilton labour history make clear, the city does not deserve its dreary reputation as a "lunchbucket town." Hamilton is no backwater of stagnant drudgery. Stirring events have kept its history flowing. Indeed, its history almost monopolizes the list of firsts in the Canadian labour movement.

True, Hamilton labour history lacks some of the cosmopolitan views, advanced causes and fringe groups that took root in more metropolitan centres like Montreal, Toronto and Vancouver. It lacks some of the clearcut socialism found in cities like Winnipeg, where radical British and European immigrants played a leading role in the labour movement. The frontier flair and bitter polarizations common to single-industry resource towns are also missing.

Hamilton nevertheless remains a banner city in the pageant of the labour movement. Hamilton workers formed the first local labour council in the 1860s. They mobilized the first Nine-Hour League in the 1870s. They elected the first of their own class to Parliament in 1872. They formed the first Canadian local of the secret Knights of Labor in 1881. They sent the first labour candidate to the provincial parliament in 1906. The first labour minister in the province was elected there in 1920. The first Cooperative Commonwealth Federation (CCF) provincial candidate was elected in Hamilton in 1934.

As the authors of these "firsts", Hamilton workers had to respond to and struggle with some of the most technologically progressive, socially sophisticated and politically astute industrialists in the country. The labour movement needed all of these qualities and more before it could survive and grow. These challenges, together with lessons learned from experiences across the country, bred a hybrid movement that could consolidate the gains of all workers.

The study of the Hamilton labour movement properly begins with the struggle for the nine-hour day in 1872. Not that strikes or protests were new by that late date; individual groups of workingmen had been fighting for decades. In the 1830s, journeymen carpenters downed their tools rather than work beside wage-cutting, semi-skilled "hammer and saw men." During the 1850s, gangs of Irish labourers took over the streets in desperate protests against starvation wages. In 1854, custom tailors launched a boycott against "the evil monster," the steam-powered sewing machine that threatened their trade. All these struggles were shortlived and limited in scope. Against this background, the nine-hour movement of 1872 marked the beginning of the labour *movement*, an ongoing struggle which involved many groups of working people in unified action, which set its sights on long range improvements in society, which left a legacy of institutions and ideas for future generations.

"Art is long, life is short," declared one of the banners in the five-mile long parade. "Wisdom is better than wealth," declared another. The nine-hour day could "elevate the social and intellectual standing of the laborer," a labour paper maintained in 1872, and "prevent his being so enervated and depressed by ceaseless toil that all the spirit and manhood is worked out of him." The nine-hour campaign kicked off a movement that was greater than the sum of its collective bargaining parts. The nine-hour pioneers did more than barter over wages and hours. They gave birth to a humanitarian movement. They wanted to improve the quality of life.

This concern for human dignity is a persistent theme in Hamilton labour history. It was echoed by Hamilton's street railway workers in 1906. Transit workers were the pioneers of unionism among the unskilled, and they wanted to "place our occupation upon a high plane of intelligence and skill... to reduce the hours of daily labour, and by all legal and proper means to elevate our moral, intellectual and social conditions." Almost 30 years later, a woman worker, exhausted by the speed-ups of the infamous "Bedaux System" in the garment trades, voiced the concern for her generation. "What the working classes want most is work," she wrote to the *Spectator* in 1935, "work they can be happy in the doing of it, with strength left for recreation."

Dignity and independence remained the intangibles of the strikes for industrial unionism in 1946, but there can be no doubt that these values underlay the key union demands for a 44 hour week and a living wage. Before 1945, fully two-thirds of the population lived below the poverty line. Until then, the market, not human need, dictated the standard of living. Industrial unionism did nothing less than insist on human standards in industry.

Concern for human dignity, together with the hard realities of working class life, prevented the labour movement from becoming just another organized vested interest group. Labour's concern for human dignity fostered a commitment to improve society that outlived any particular union campaign. That commitment was central to the popularity of the Knights of Labor during the 1880s, and then outlasted the Knights as well. In the twentieth century, that commitment was translated into successful political action. Four days after the dust had cleared from the 1906 transit strike, the former Knight of Labor, Allan Studholme, was elected to the legislature as a labour representative of the community. Two years after a combination of employers delivered a bloody nose to union machinists in 1917, Hamilton electors sent a slate of labour representatives to the legislature. Thereafter, independent labour political action became a fixture of local and provincial elections.

Thus, the heritage of the nineteenth century labour movement filtered through the dust and smoke of the factory town that Hamilton became after 1900. There has been a tendency to disown that heritage. Its legacy has been distorted by the bitter controversy that raged between craft and industrial unionists during the 1930s and 1940s. The craft tradition curdled and went sour when it was left outside the huge factories of the twentieth century. Nevertheless, the continuing and vital contribution of skilled workers steeped in an artisanal tradition cannot be overlooked. To gain a more balanced perspective, we have but to consider Sam Lawrence, the old-fashioned stonecutter and craft unionist of pre-World War I days who became a principal architect of successful industrial unionism in Hamilton.

The labour movement, itself one of the major spurs to social change in Canada, also had to change itself to meet new challenges. This did not mean that workers had to forget all they ever knew. Sheet mill workers at Stelco showed how events could revitalize traditional approaches, when they became central figures in the transition to industrial unionism after 1935. The sheet mill workers may have been semi-skilled by comparison with artisans of the nineteenth century, but they still commanded skills and work habits that harkened back to an earlier time. Perhaps this gave them the self-confidence to challenge an industrial giant like Stelco in the midst of the Depression. The sheet mill workers also maintained the old initiation rites and observances common to the nineteenth century, when workers joined unions as a result of an intensely personal decision, not as a result of a union check-off agreement. Milton Montgomery, active in the 1935 strike and later a Steelworkers' organizer, remembered how these rituals made a union man profoundly aware of his obligations to fellow workers. When the sheet mill workers were unable to win their demands in 1935, they quickly turned toward industrial unionism and sustained the union drive at Stelco for another 11 years.

Change did not always flow as smoothly. The artisanal heritage could not help Hamilton's factory workers in the Hamilton labour force after 1900. The Canadian workforce, unlike the workforce of other countries, is composed almost entirely of immigrants. Until 1900, most immigrants to Hamilton were Anglo-Saxon. After 1900, large numbers came from southern and eastern Europe. Uniting these various ethnic groups in a common cause was the most difficult and perhaps the greatest accomplishment of the Hamilton labour movement. It was achieved by Hamilton workers themselves, long before "multiculturalism" became public policy or acceptable in polite society.

To achieve this unity, Hamilton unionists had to confront one of the basic social mechanisms of Hamilton industry. Hamilton city fathers were not so crude as to follow in the footsteps of one western Canadian city which established a suburb, "Toil Incorporated," specifically for immigrant industrial workers. Nevertheless, Hamilton's immigrants were forcefully segregated, in both jobs and homes. Italians were prohibited by law from living in fashionable Westdale. Italians and other continental European immigrants were given only the dirtiest, least stable jobs in heavy industry.

This system of ethnic segregation, suggested Harold Keeton, formerly of the United Rubber Workers in Hamilton, performed two functions. First, it gave Anglo-Saxon workers a false sense of superiority. Secondly, it kept workers "in line," ever fearful that the employer might "open the floodgates" to a large reserve of labour, should the Anglo-Saxon workers ever protest. The companies "had a more captive workforce that way," Keeton reflected, "and they could turn the screws a bit more."

Hamilton workers were not able to tackle this and other problems until World War II. As a city of heavy industry, Hamilton has always been subject to all the ups and downs of the world economy. In the years from 1907 to 1909, 1913 to 1915, 1920 to 1925, 1929 to 1939, this had meant depression, severe competition for jobs, and a downturn in the labour movement. In the years from 1915 to 1918 and 1939 to 1945, when goods were produced for war and full employment resulted, the labour movement made its gains. These gains were tested after World War I, when recession, aggressive counter-organizing by employers and demoralization whittled away all the wartime gains. After World War II, however, the labour movement held its own.

The strikes of 1946 took place at a historic moment in Canadian history. The wartime gains of unions seemed fragile. The country was preparing for reconstruction. Would it be reconstructed on a union basis? Industy's captains, sensing the time had come to tame their rambunctious workers once and for all, folded their arms and swaggered. Labour took the dare.

Workers had been preparing for this moment for 75 years. A glance at some of the people involved reveals the inheritance the strikers enjoyed, the breadth of resources that unions were able to draw on.

For the steelworkers, there was Local 1005 President, Reg Gardiner. As a farmboy, Gardiner fell heir to the traditions of agrarian co-operation and Christian socialism that dated back to the 1890s. There was Vice-President George Martin, first drawn to the labour movement by the wave of labour unrest in 1919. There was steward Tony Gervasio, who in 1942 found unionism to be the only guarantee against ethnic discrimination. Organizer Larry Sefton was a veteran of the bitter Kirkland Lake strike of 1941-2, a strike that developed out of the traditions of the old Western Federation of Miners and One Big Union. Negotiations were conducted by Charlie Millard, leader of the Oshawa auto-workers' strike of 1937 that created the first successful industrial union in Canada.

At Westinghouse, there was Alf Ready, a typical product of Hamilton's North End, and Ernie Koko, first radicalized by the brutal civil war in his native Finland. These two builders of the UE were first brought together through the efforts of the Hunter and McClure brothers, all hailing from Scotland and brought into

Communist Party activity by the unemployment that ravaged young working class suburbanites on Hamilton Mountain during the 1930s.

In the broader realm of the labour movement, there was Jim Stowe, practising the almost artisanal craft of patternmaking and serving as President of the Hamilton Labor Council. Stowe had been President of the Newfoundland Federation of Labour before migrating to Hamilton during the war. From the other side of the country came Harvey Ladd, fresh from a decade's experience with CCF clubs, miners, and lumbermen in British Columbia. Ladd came to Hamilton during the war to help solidify a stewards' movement through the Workers' Educational Association. Finally, there was Sam Lawrence, the old-country stonecutter who became a socialist while serving in the trenches during the Boer War. Lawrence put his decades of service as a craft unionist and labour politician at the disposal of industrial unionism.

What did Hamilton workers win after the long, hot summer of 1946? Workers used their newly aroused solidarity to create new industrial unions, new methods of dealing with grievances, and new standards of living.

The scale of these victories was not so apparent just after the conflict subsided. Employers exaggerated it. "Since the war," Hamilton lawyer D.L.G. Jones bellowed in 1949, "the unions have been attempting to enter in equal share in management of industry and have now entered the field of social services. Their union halls are another bid to establish their influence with the workers. Whereas a man formerly went to his minister or member of Parliament for advice or help," Jones terrified his audience, "he now goes to the union hall. Here he can procure the services of a lawyer to fight an eviction. They will back his note in order that it will be honoured at the bank and they will intercede with the police if a union member happens to have an erring son. This can lead to a labour party in Canada."

The labour movement has not always lived up to those challenges. Now a new generation of workers must take them up. When they do, they will stand on the shoulders of countless numbers of rank and file activists who went before them. Their achievements are chronicled in the pages to come.

VOL. V.—No. 23.            MONTREAL, SATURDAY, JUNE 8, 1872.          {SINGLE COPIES, TEN CENTS. / $4 PER YEAR IN ADVANCE.

The nine-hour demonstration in Hamilton, May 15, 1872.

# The Nine-Hour Pioneers

*Honour the men of Hamilton,*
*The Nine-Hour pioneers,*
*Their memory will be kept green,*
*Throughout the coming years.*
*And every honest son of toil*
*That lives in freedom's light*
*Shall bless that glorious day in May*
*When might gave way to right.*

*Alexander Wingfield*

It was a splendid day in May 1872 when Hamilton's wage-earners marched out of their workshops to demand the nine-hour day. Carrying colourful flags and banners, 1,500 men paraded through the city. To entertain the well-wishers who lined the streets to cheer them on, each group of craftsmen proudly displayed the tools and products of its craft. Later, massive crowds thronged to the Crystal Palace to hear speeches about the dignity of labour and the rights of the workingman. On that sunny spring day, Hamilton led off Canada's first great demonstration of working class solidarity in the emerging age of industrial capitalism.

Four months earlier, Hamilton machinists and blacksmiths had kicked off the movement to create a Nine-Hours League. Most of the city's tradesmen joined this campaign. They wanted to equalize the benefits of new industrial processes by shortening the hours of work. One of the League's leaders, James Ryan, described how "the capitalist had profited by the labour and toil of his workmen, while the workmen themselves had not received a corresponding profit." Workers, he insisted, "should share with the capitalist in the advantages of machinery." This pioneer union leader also stressed the dignity of labour. He saw the nine-hour day as the only way to secure the gains of democracy. The 55-hour week, under the gruelling pace set by factory taskmasters, threatened the workers' rights to read and think and to exercise their rights and obligations as reponsible citizens. "We want not more *money*, but more *brains*; not richer serfs, but better *men*," Ryan emphasized.

Other Nine-Hours Leagues throughout southern Ontario sent delegates to Hamilton that May to form the Canadian Labor Protective and Mutual Improvement Association. It was Canada's first regional labour federation.

The bosses, however, were also organizing. Winning the nine-hour day meant fighting local employers. In Toronto, the *Globe's* George Brown and fellow publishers battled with printers over the issue. In Hamilton, employers locked out supporters of the nine-hour day in early May. By the end of the month, most workers had to recognize defeat and return to work on the old terms. It took another 75 years before most Hamilton workers won relief from inhumanly long hours of toil.

The Nine-Hour campaign, however, had one unexpected result. Taking advantage of the popular mood, the local Conservatives nominated a workingman for a seat in the House of Commons — Henry Buckingham Witton, a foreman in the Great Western Railway paint shop, who had not been prominent in the shorter-hours agitation. In August 1872, workers' votes helped make him the country's first workingman in Parliament.

Witton's performance as the workers' mouthpiece in the House was lacklustre. By 1873, the governor-general's wife saw a change in him. "We had met him soon after his election when he dined in a rough coat," she remembered with disgust, "but now he wears evening clothes. He talked so pleasantly..." In 1874, Witton lost his seat along with so many of Sir John A. Macdonald's Conservatives.

Witton eventually became a successful businessman and a leader in the campaign for a public library at the end of the century. But a poem published in a local newspaper in 1875 revealed his tarnished reputation with Hamilton workers:

*The workingman who gets a lift*
*Above his fellow's head,*
*Too often proves no more a friend*
*To those who toil for bread.*

*The independence labor won*
*Is quickly flung away —*
*His "fellow-workingmen" forgot*
*Till next election day.*

*His sympathies with titles run —*
*A toady now as then —*
*His clap-trap is by far "too thin"*
*To gull the workingmen.*

# The Knights of Labour

They called it the Noble and Holy Order of the Knights of Labor — surely the most elegant name ever to grace a labour organization in Hamilton. The Knights began in 1869 as a small secret society of Philadelphia garment cutters. Soon the Order spread throughout North America, to Britain and Australia. At its peak, it claimed more than 700,000 members across the world. Hamilton workers once again became Canadian pioneers when 40 painters met in an unfinished building in 1881 to form Canada's first active Knights assembly.

For workers in the late nineteenth century, this peculiar labour body successfully blended the old and the new. Members memorized an elaborate set of handhakes and passwords modelled on rituals from the popular fraternal societies. Officials with exalted titles like "Master Workman" and "Venerable Sage" presided over their meetings. Greeting a fellow Knight on the street, a member would announce, "I am a worker." His mate would respond: "I too earn my bread by the sweat of my brow." Elaborate gestures preceded and followed.

Although all this ritual now seems archaic and ridiculous, it was appropriate enough at the time. Unions had only recently won legal status, and employers'

opposition made secrecy necessary. Furthermore, the ritual expressed a sense of intimacy and belonging to a cause. It was part of the Knights' reassertion of the dignity that impersonal industrial capitalism was stripping from Hamilton's artisans.

Moreover, the Knights based their appeal on a modern sense of solidarity among wage-earners, who were beginning to recognize that workers were an exploited class. The Order aimed to speak for "the producers," who needed an organization to rescue society from the parasitic "monopolists." The Knights' sense of class led them to fling their doors open to both skilled and unskilled workers, including women and blacks. "An injury to one is the conern of all," was their motto.

Not content to devote their entire attention to "bread and butter" issues, the Knights stressed labour education. Each local assembly became a sounding board for the discussion of trade and social problems. Even though a fledgling movement, the Knights produced lively local newspapers, first the *Labor Union* and later the *Palladium of Labor*. Political action, they believed, was the best route for social change. In 1883, 1886, and 1887, the Order ran independent labour candidates for local office. All three campaigns fell short of victory at the polls.

As unionists, the Knights had an uneven record. They led some important strikes against the city's most stubborn employers. But the Knights' leaders generally opposed strikes. They relied instead on the good will of negotiators or arbitrators. Disgusted with this hesitation to lead strike action, many workers turned to the craft unions of the American Federation of Labor.

In 1887, the Knights of Labor organized more than 2,000 people in the city, represented in 31 local assemblies and co-ordinated by a District Assembly. Sucess was short-lived, however. Employers gave the Knights no quarter. Craft unions competed to represent skilled workers. Conflict turned inward and factional intrigue boiled over. By 1888, the Knights' membership had evaporated.

The Knights had led the most successful attempt to unite Hamilton working people in the nineteenth century. They levelled sharp criticisms at the inhumanity of the emerging industrial order and argued repeatedly for wholesale political and social change. They wanted to build a co-operative economic system to replace the grinding competion of capitalism, and even attempted a few experiments with co-operative stores and workshops.

John Peebles, a mayor of Hamilton in the 1930s, looked back kindly on the high idealism of his youthful years in the Knights. "I thought its program would revolutionize the world, not only because of... co-operative and state ownership of all public utilities," he reminisced. "It was a crusade for purity in life generally."

# The Craftsmen's Council

Unionism took a new lease on life at the turn of the century. The prolonged depression that capped the nineteenth century had finally ended. A burst of prosperity gave birth to a hardy new brand of unionism. Beginning in the late 1890s, thousands of Canadian workers flocked into the craft unions of the American Federation of Labor. The AFL unions promised full-time organizers, a solid financial structure, protection for the journeyman's status and a chance to work throughout the continent, wherever the union had a branch. In 1900 John Flett, a Hamilton carpenter and former Knight of Labor, became the AFL's first Canadian organizer. Two years later, Flett was elected president of the Canadian Trades and Labor Congress, at a convention which expelled the last of the Knights' assemblies and any other competing organizations.

Each craft union protected its own jurisdiction. But it also joined in common organizations to promote the interests of workingmen and of the community at large. The craftsmen's collective voice in Hamilton was the Hamilton Trades and Labor Council, founded in 1888. Before 1914, local councils like this became the key agencies of the Canadian labour movement. They were close to the day-to-day concerns of workers, and they were able to act quickly and on a wide range of issues.

Twice a month, delegates from most Hamilton craft unions — plumbers, bricklayers, carpenters, barbers, moulders, and so on — met to mull over important issues for local workers. The council usually left each craft to organize and defend itself, but an Organization Committee did occasionally pitch in to help. A Union Label League also tried to convince local merchants to stock union-made goods. Each fall, the council hosted a festival of speeches and entertainment to celebrate Labour Day.

Starting in 1912, Hamilton workers could follow local labour movement activities in the columns of a lively weekly labour paper, the *Labor News*. Samuel Landers, a former clothing worker in the city and once an official in the United Garment Workers, edited the paper.

The Hamilton labour movement tried to keep the city's voters interested in a broad platform of principles, well ahead of the times. The labour programme emphasized both economic measures to improve the lot of workers and political reforms to strengthen and expand democratic government. These craft unionists wanted public ownership of all utilities, abolition of the contract system in public work, and curbs on pauper immigration. They wanted equal pay and equal voting rights for women, an end to war, and the abolition of the Senate. And they wanted "national insurance of working people against accidents, lack of employment, and want in old age."

The shorter working day also remained a priority. "When men invented machines to do the work in shorter hours," a Hamilton patternmaker told a royal commission in 1910, "they ought to reap the benefit in shorter hours and a few of the pleasures of life." The printers won the first victory in 1905. Five years later,

twelve local crafts boasted that they worked an eight-hour day.

Not all the traditions of craft unionism, however, meshed well with the new conditions of industrial life in Hamilton. The craftsmen jealously guarded their separate union jurisdictions and refused to promote a strategy to unite all workers in the same industry into one union. In 1912 the Trades and Labour Council voted down a resolution favouring industrial unionism.

Most of the council's membership was based in industries producing goods and services for the working class consumer. Tailors, broommakers, stovemounters and

building tradesmen worked in small shops and often could overcome employer resistance by appealing to working class consumers to buy union-label goods. But an organizing strategy based on small shops, traditional skills and the union label overlooked the thousands of unorganized workers in the new iron and steel plants. These huge and centralized corporations rarely manufactured products directly for a consumer market. As a result, the needs of unskilled workers were ignored by the old craft strategy. The unskilled had to fight their own sporadic battles in the city's factories without support from the organized bastions of the labour movement.

A Labour Day parade celebrates Hamilton's centennial, 1913.

TRADES AND LABOR PARADE        HAMILTON CENTENIAL

A street car and the company office, following a visit by crowds of strike supporters.

Street car en route to Car Sheds after encounter with mob during strike.

# We Walk to Win

Ten thousand men and women cursing, shoving, and pitching rocks. Mounted soldiers charging through the crowds. The mayor reading the Riot Act. Does this sound like Hamilton? For four weeks in November 1906, thousands of Hamilton's working people milled through the downtown streets in the most powerful strike support action the city ever witnessed before 1946.

It all began with a dispute on the Hamilton Street Railway. The motormen and conductors on the street cars organized a union in 1899. By August 1906, they were on a collision course with the Hamilton Street Railway Company, a private monopoly in charge of the city's public transit. When negotiations ran into a dead end, arbitrators moved in and gave the workers what they wanted in higher wages and shorter hours. The company initially gave in, but then renounced the arbitrators' award in late October.

On November 4, all 180 street railway workers walked off the job. Within days, skilled workers in the repair shops and non-unionized workers on the suburban radial lines joined in. The company promptly declared its intention to drive out the union.

It soon became clear that the company had angered more than its workers. The street railway's tracks ran throughout the city and provided transportation for most of Hamilton's population. Riders resented being jammed into dilapidated cars and found the service "abominable," according to the *Spectator*. The very autumn of the strike, the city council dragged the company before the Ontario Railway and Municipal Board.

Working people harboured a special grudge against Cataract Power, the large corporation which owned the street railway. The corporation became the target of the smouldering resentment against the big new monopolies which were taking charge of the country. One worker expressed his feelings in poetic form:

> *They care not for the citizens,*
> *Nor for the city's rights;*
> *To make enormous dividends*
> *Is always their delight.*

Small wonder, then, that the population sided with the strikers. Everyone began sporting little blue "We Walk" ribbons. "Walking," chirped the *Spectator*, "is fine exercise."

When the company imported outsiders, mostly ruffians, to man and protect the street cars, community support for the strikers swept through the city. Noisy parades, huge mass meetings, special church services, and benefit concerts showed the depth of public feeling. As tempers flared at the obstinacy of the company, violence erupted. Angry crowds swarmed over the company property. Choosing their targets carefully, the crowds pelted the car barns and street cars with rocks and bottles and harassed strikebreakers and security guards. Businessmen who dared to openly support the company had their windows smashed. A stick of dynamite blew the roof off the company building. Barricades were built on the tracks to derail any cars put into service. On one radial line, guns blazed. Violence came to a head on November 23, when the company again refused to negotiate. A ferocious attack by thousands of citizens overwhelmed city police. City

fathers panicked and summoned the militia from Toronto and London. The following night, the mayor read the Riot Act. Policemen and mounted soldiers broke up the huge crowds with batons and sabres.

The next day, "scores of citizens" were "laid up with grievous bodily injuries," and the *Spectator* blamed the violence and injuries on "police fury, and some think, indiscretion." The city continued to show its hostility. The troops had to face insults on the streets and in letters to the newspapers. Teamsters even refused to deliver goods to them. The police added insult to injury by trying to deport the organizer for the street railwaymen's union, Fred Fay.

In this tense atmosphere of a strike-bound city, the company finally agreed to let the provincial Railway and Municipal

Board arbitrate. On November 30, the strikers returned to work. The board announced its decision one week later, and forced the street railway workers to swallow a bitter pill. The company would have to recognize the union and sign a three-year contract, but the workers got no wage increase. Bitterness lingered on, but in future years there were no more strikes on Hamilton's street car lines.

The strike also had lasting effects on local politics. The dust had not even cleared when, in a provincial by-election for the East Hamilton seat held four days after the strike ended, Allan Studholme became the city's first independent labour parliamentarian. One month later, several labour candidates also won seats on city council. In the same election, Hamilton voters defied the arrogant Cataract company and endorsed publicly owned hydro-electric power facilities.

# The Little Stovemounter

"Just show me what you have done for the class I represent, the most important class in the province, the wage-earners," cried the short, white-haired figure with the little black cap. The year was 1911, and the sedate legislative chamber at Queen's Park echoed again with the hard-hitting rhetoric of Hamilton's small but spunky labour member, Allan Studholme. For thirteen years, this lone voice of labour in the House made life difficult for men on the government's front benches.

Studholme was born in 1846 near Birmingham, England. He worked at farm labouring and other odd jobs before immigrating to Canada in 1870. In Dundas, Ontario, he learned the trade of stove-mounting, the assembling of cast-iron stoves.

In the 1880s, he joined the Knights of Labor and became an active unionist in Hamilton. When the city's foundry owners blacklisted him he took over the management of a co-operative grocery store run by the Knights.

A serious accident forced him to recuperate in Australia and New Zealand for several years. But he was back in the thick of Hamilton labour activity by the turn of the century. In 1903 and 1904 he was elected international president of the Stove Mounters' Union.

The street railway strike of 1906 brought Studholme further into the limelight, since he acted for the workers on the arbitration board. That same fall, a convention of trade unionists nominated him to run as an independent labour candidate in the East Hamilton by-election. He rode to office on the wave of solidarity created by the strike, to become Ontario's first independent labourite in the legislature. Through three more elections, he was unbeatable.

As the only labour man in the House, Studholme became the "Labor Party" at Queen's Park. He consistently refused to make any deals with the old-line parties. Like Keir Hardie in Britain, he defiantly donned a small cloth workingman's cap when he entered the House.

Studholme shocked and outraged establishment politicians. His energy and flair were remarkable considering that he was already 60 years old when he entered politics. He was always on his feet criticizing government measures that catered to privilege, violated democratic practices, or endangered workers. He lashed out at government funding to assist immigration from Britain, since he believed that the Canadian labour market was being deliberately flooded. He stood guard over the province's first workmen's compensation legislation against attacks from manufacturers. In the House and on public platforms, he campaigned for public ownership of hydro-electric power, which the local Dominion Power and Transmission Company fought tooth and nail.

He was also the champion of women's suffrage and each year sponsored bills to give women the right to vote and sit in the legislature. Thanks to the old-line parties' command of the House, Studholme's motions seldom found a seconder. But Studholme was undaunted. Like J.S. Woodsworth in the 1920s, he used his position as a platform for proclaiming a labour programme of social and political reform.

Behind Studholme stood the Hamilton Independent Labor Party. The party's programme accented immediate issues related to political democracy and social security, rather than a full socialist platform. Recognized as the strongest local labour organization in the province, the ILP missed electing a second member by only 36 votes in 1914.

# The Best Men We Have

Hamilton's labour history is not a story of working *men* only. In 1884 Henry George, a popular American labour reformer, broke off the text of his speech to a rally of Hamilton workers and declared that "the most striking feature in that procession of yours today was the ladies — the women of your society." A wisecracker quickly shouted from the floor: "The women are the best men we have."

Women did not always get so much attention in Hamilton's labour movement. In fact, few of them found their way onto the membership rolls of the unions, or into the smoky meetings of the Hamilton Trades and Labor Council.

Their generally unskilled jobs, of course, made them difficult to organize before the rise of mass industrial unionism. Women also had only short stints in the paid work force, since most quit work for good when they married.

The attitude of local labour leaders did not help either. They spent little time organizing female workers and expected the "working girls" to head back to their proper place as homemakers. No female delegate appeared at a trades and labour council meeting until 1918, when Sadie Walker presented her credentials from the Retail Clerks' Union.

Most often, male trade unionists in the city steered women toward two roles on the sidelines of the labour movement. In one role, as ladies' auxiliaries, they served cake and ice cream at union social functions. According to one woman organizer, auxiliaries were busy "backing up the men in many various ways in their struggle for improved working conditions."

In another role, women could do the family shopping with an eye out for union-label goods. "The wives and daughters of union men will exert an immense influence in the near future in the industrial struggle," the *Industrial Banner* noted in 1905. The paper recommended that unions "lose no time in bringing the women folks into line by the formation of Label Leagues."

Women wage-earners joined unions in industries where they were hired in large numbers and where male workers could take the lead. The Knights of Labor had briefly organized female workers in shoe and textile mills. After 1900, unions in the local shoe and tobacco plants included all the women employees. But these were only a tiny fraction of the female work force.

Organization of women in the more important clothing and textile industries began in 1913. That year nearly 1,500 women in the four largest clothing factories joined the United Garment Workers of America and marched out on strike for higher wages. An air of excitement hung over the streets, as the young women discovered the solidarity of the picket line. "I was never on strike before!" one of them joked with a crowd of girl friends. "Gee, but it's lots of fun, isn't it?" After two weeks they won a modest wage increase, but the union collapsed within a year. At the end of World War I, the Amalgamated Clothing Workers swept up all the women in the city's clothing factories.

At the same time, some women in the cotton mills turned to the United Textile Workers and the One Big Union. Both these organizations collapsed in the early 1920s, but the Textile Workers bounced back in 1929 during a bitter, unsuccessful strike against the introduction of scientific management and speed-ups at the Canadian Cottons plant.

A few courageous heroines of the labour movement rallied their sisters for these struggles. Katie McVicar, a shoe worker whose talents for organizing helped establish the first Canadian women's assembly of the Knights of Labor in 1884, was the earliest example. In her footsteps followed Mary McNab, who accepted the mantle of secretary and business agent for the new clothing workers' local during World War I.

Hamilton's women also plunged into labour politics. When Ontario granted them the vote in 1917, the wives of the local ILP leaders founded a Women's Independent Labor Party, with social and educational programmes specifically for women. In 1920, many of these same women helped to form the Women's Educational Federation of Ontario. This new body campaigned for "the education of women on all social and political questions affecting their interests." It drew half its executive from Hamilton. In 1924, a group of Hamilton women activists banded together as the Women's Labor League.

These new women's labour groups tried to bridge the worlds of working women, wives and mothers. To the general labour movement goals of the eight-hour day and a minimum wage, they added maternity leave, free medical care during pregnancy, and better education and health provisions for children.

Mary McNab captured the mood of these Hamilton women. "It is well known," she wrote in 1921, "that woman of today has new ideals, new moral conceptions, new methods of action, the justice of which has given her the courage of her convictions. But leave her alone, and when she has set the house of the nation to rights she will reappear in the next generation (as) man's ideal woman."

In 1913 the unionized women workers at the McPherson shoe factory waved from their float during a labour parade.

Dr. Brown—

We the maids of the General Hospital under Mrs. Smith. are demanding a $5.00 increase a month in pay. Unless we hear definitely by Wed. 13th. at 9 o'clock, we are all through.— We will be at Mrs. Smith office 9 o'Clock sharp

This undated letter of protest, found in the records of the Hamilton General Hospital, may be typical of unpublicized confrontations between women workers and their employers. Women could and did resist poor working conditions, but they had trouble sustaining permanent organizations.

# The Patriotism of Profits

*Generals Die in Bed* was the title a Canadian veteran gave to his novel on the "Great War" of 1914-1918. Workers did not have it so easy.

Hamilton was in the grip of war fever from the outset. The city's population contained thousands of British immigrants; their enlistment in the Canadian Expeditionary Force was brisk. In July 1915 war enthusiasts in Hamilton created the country's first Recruiting League to keep the young men flooding into the ranks.

According to one League official, "no man could escape the eloquent appeals that caught his eye at every turn. He could not walk ten yards or read ten minutes without some startling reminder that he had a duty to his empire." Eventually, prodded by such hoopla, every ninth citizen signed up to fight — some 11,000 in all. The city boasted one of the highest rates of enlistment in the country.

Behind the lines, Hamilton also fought, though not always with the enemy abroad. The city was a centre of munitions production for the Allies. Almost every metal shop in town converted to making shells for the Allied guns.

The soaring cost of living and the long hours of feverishly-paced work soon stirred up discontent among the city's workers. The machinists' union had no trouble signing up hundreds of munitions workers. By the spring of 1916, it confronted the employers with demands for better wages and shorter hours. The federal government hastily appointed a royal commission. But the commission's recommendations for higher wages and a nine-hour day were flatly rejected by the "open-shop" companies.

The union had to face a militant new Employers Association. The companies tried to whip up hysteria. Huge newspaper ads charged that the trouble had been "engineered from a foreign country where agitators had been so active in exploiting the cause of our enemies." Civic politicians and local clergymen met late into the night in a frantic effort to mediate the conflict. But the companies refused to make any concessions. On June 12, some 1,500 exasperated workers walked out of the munitions plants.

"The manufacturers are trying to turn the crank so as to squeeze a little more out of the workingman," one striker was overheard to grumble. "The patriotism of the manufacturer is represented by the single word 'profits,'" another snarled.

Using its wartime powers, the federal government imposed a news blackout to keep the conflict from spreading. With no newspaper reports and disunity in the ranks of the workers, the dispute quietly died at the end of the summer. Many of the strikers tramped off to find better jobs elsewhere. It had been the biggest strike of the Canadian munitions industry in World War I. Once again, it had also been a defeat for Hamilton's workers' efforts to win a shorter working day.

Full employment and a shortage of labour gave many other workers the chance to protest more effectively. By 1919, Hamilton's wage-earners had created the biggest labour movement in thirty years. Old craft unions came to life with new vigour. New industrial unions sprang up among textile, garment, steel, and meatpacking workers. Even a branch of the radical One Big Union flourished briefly in the city.

"The workers have a new vision," a Hamilton blacksmith announced to a royal commission in 1919; "today the workers are not only demanding shorter hours and better working conditions, but they seem to want a higher standard of living entirely..."

Unfortunately, a new depression in 1920 brought down the curtain on this burst of labour organization. Not until the full employment of the next World War would Hamilton's working people recover the economic leverage to press their demand for "a higher standard of living."

# A New Democracy

"We are standing today upon the threshold of a new age, on the threshold of a new democracy that is beginning to demand dignity and freedom..." So wrote Fred Flatman in 1919 in the first editorial of a new labour newspaper in Hamilton, optimistically titled *New Democracy*. He recognized that "there is lying beneath all the labour unrest that is manifesting itself throughout the entire world today a healthy desire for higher and greater things."

Hamilton workers' hopes for a new and better postwar world flowed into independent labour politics. The first ILP alderman had been elected in 1915. He was a plumber, George Halcrow. Another ILP alderman and a school trustee joined him the next year. In 1917, in the famous conscription election when Robert Borden's Unionists ran up stunning majorities in English Canada, ILP candidates in Hamilton were among the few labour representatives in the country who did not lose their deposits.

The big breakthrough for the party came in 1919. ILP branches in West Hamilton, Dundas, East Hamilton, Mount Hamilton, and Barton Township were thriving. The Central branch alone had 1,200 dues-paying supporters by the end of the year. In January 1919 municipal voters elected two controllers, five aldermen, a school trustee, and a hydro-electric commissioner from the ILP slate. The labour candidate for mayor lost in 1920 and 1921, but another labour alderman won a seat in these elections.

As usual, Hamilton was leading a movement of regional and national momentum. In 1917 local labour leaders helped create a province-wide Independent Labor Party. Two years later the party's Hamilton branch swept both local seats in a provincial election. George Halcrow and Walter Rollo, a fomer broommaker and now a newspaperman, joined Premier E.C. Drury's Farmer-Labor coalition; Rollo became a leader of the eleven-man Labor caucus. Drury also named him minister of labour — the first time workers in Ontario were treated seriously enough to have their own ministry.

All was not well inside Hamilton's labour party, however. The return of depression and unemployment in 1920 sapped the strength of local labour organizations. The momentum of confidence and optimism among workers soon began to falter.

Internal wrangles, especially over the coalition with the farmers, disrupted party life. The farmers' leaders had always been reluctant to support labour goals like the eight-hour day and a high tariff to protect industrial jobs. In 1923 Hamilton's George Halcrow broke away in protest to run as an independent. The vagueness of ILP ideology and the undistinguished record of some of the party's elected men also posed problems. Many of them sounded little different from the other parties.

Most ILP politicians lost their seats in the early 1920s — with one significant exception. Out in the east end, in Ward 8, a popular young stonecutter named Sam Lawrence held on as an ILP alderman. In 1928, he went on to win a seat on the Board of Control. Hamilton would hear much more from this man, whom the *Herald* described as "a good platform speaker, of unflinching courage and convincing straightforwardness."

The rise and fall of Hamilton's Independent Labor Party was not the last chapter in the story of labour politics in the city. Remnants of the party hung on and joined the Co-operative Commonwealth Federation in the 1930s.

# Red Unionism

"Communists and Reds are at the bottom of the trouble and wages have nothing to do with it." The manager of the National Steel Car plant in Hamilton muttered these words to a reporter in 1929, during one of Hamilton's most tumultuous strikes of the 1920s. It was a major event in the evolution of industrial unionism in the city.

Marxian socialists had hovered on the fringes of the Hamilton labour movement since the 1890s. They had harshly criticized narrow craft unionism and had championed all-embracing industrial unionism with a strong political commitment.

Their first experiment with industrial unionism was a branch of the Industrial Workers of the World, formed in 1908. This group quickly dissolved. In 1919 another group tried to build support for the One Big Union, which had wide support in western Canada. Once again the radicals failed. The IWW and OBU locals in Hamilton were never more than propaganda committees to spread the ideas of militant industrial unionism. Neither succeeded in leading any group of workers in a strike.

During the 1920s, many Canadian socialists joined the Communist Party. In the late twenties, the Communists began to promote independent, industrial unions. The situation in 1929 at the National Steel Car Corporation offered an excellent opportunity for this new unionism, which blossomed into the Workers' Unity League a few months later.

National Steel Car turned out railway cars in one of the city's most modern mass production plants. From its earliest days, the company had filled its factory with European immigrants and had driven them hard. In July 1929, a worker reported: "Not enough that they get practically nothing for the most intense labor, the workers here are forced to work 12-13 hours on the night shift and 10-12 hours on the day shift." Often they worked seven days without a break.

In 1929, the company installed new equipment, re-organized the work in the plant, and cut piece rates. On September 4, over 400 riveters walked off the job to protest these changes, which reduced their earnings by 40 to 50 per cent. After only one conference, the company refused to meet the strikers again.

As the strike began, the workers formed the National Steel Car Workers' Industrial Union, with an initial membership of over 500. The union drafted a list of concrete demands: a minimum wage of $40 a week, time and a half for overtime, the eight-hour day, abolition of piece-work, improved safety measures, dining room facilities, and better heating in the plant.

For the next six weeks, the strikers fought running battles with the company, police, scabs, city officials, and craft unionists. Mass meetings and mass pickets confronted 45 policemen at the plant gates. Police kept the plant open and occasionally arrested pickets for intimidating strikebreakers.

For the public, the presence of Communists in the union executive overshadowed all other issues. The company used the leaders' politics as a pretext to avoid bargaining. The city council refused to let the union hold a tag day to raise funds. "We should stamp out this communist menace as we would a diphtheria epidemic," thundered Mayor W. Burton. The Hamilton Trades and Labor Council, never fond of Communists or industial unionism, refused to support the strike. City newspapers denounced the new "red" unionism.

With all these forces against it, the strike collapsed in mid-October. A week later, the stock market crash heralded the deep depression which crippled union organizing for another decade. When industrial unionism finally arrived in Hamilton in the early years of World War II, however, the National Steel Car workers once again led the way.

# The Dirty Thirties

The Depression sent Hamilton reeling. No worker was spared. How could it be otherwise in the industrial capital of Canada, a city whose fortunes were fatally linked to the topsy-turvy cycles of a world economy in crisis?

Barely into the new year, the *Spectator* announced the grim news. "Unemployment Has Become Very Acute," the January 10, 1930 issue headlined. Some 800 men had registered for jobs at the city employment office. Another 1,200 men and 800 women signed up at the Ontario Employment Bureau's Hamilton office. By summer, 6,000 to 7,000 unemployed joined the endless line-ups for some kind of work.

Unknown to most Hamiltonians, these dark realities only foreshadowed the dawn of a decade-long Depression. Despite business and government blind faith that "recovery is just around the corner," the economy continued on its downward slide. It did not bottom out until 1933. Matters did not improve until the destruction of war was unleashed in 1939. The generation that suffered through that bitter decade gave it a name — The Dirty Thirties.

Employers took advantage of people's desperate search for any kind of job by driving down wages and speeding up production. In 1931, construction contractors provoked a strike of once proud and mighty building tradesmen by introducing a wage-cut of 25 cents an hour. Governments followed suit. Contractors on civic projects regularly paid their labourers below the legal 55 cents-an-hour minimum. In 1930, the Trades and Labor Council protested that a married man with five children worked 40 hours for $9.97 — 19½ cents an hour. "You were just a commodity," steelworker Harry Pomeroy declared.

The power of employers made organizing hopeless. Future labour leader Johnny Shipperbottom remembered how foremen sneered at any who dared complain: "Anytime you don't like it, there's the gate." As usual, immigrants were more vulnerable than anyone. Many had to buy their jobs with a bribe. To hold on to their jobs, just as many had to kick-back part of their wages to the foremen.

There was no legislative shield against these abuses. Unemployment insurance did not exist. City relief was doled out on a miserly basis, and only after a humiliating procedure. Thus Hamiltonians looked to each other for help. There was nowhere else to go.

Backyard gardens sprang up across the

city. Local churches and community organizations provided food, clothing and entertainment. "Man-a-block" organizations canvassed neighbourhoods for part-time jobs. During the harvest season, men bicycled to nearby farms to pick fruit and vegetables. On their way home, they had to ride past snooping city officials who stationed themselves to spot any culprits who earned some wages in addition to their meagre relief allowance. Anyone caught had his relief cut accordingly.

Just surviving was an ordeal. Families scavenged coal thrown from passing trains. They moved in the dark of night to avoid the landlord and his rent collector. They waited at the soup kitchen door for a meal and sometimes a bed. Unemployment figures of 25% were small comfort.

For most, there was little to do but wait. In the depths of the Depression, people bided their time. When the time came, they built a labour movement for keeps.

"Breadline," a 1930s woodcut by Leonard Hutchinson.

# Artists of the Crash

Leonard Hutchinson could look out of his studio on King Street and see unemployed men killing time in Gore Park or standing in line at the soup kitchens. "It was depressing," he remembered many years later. "It was terrible. ...Those poor guys, I could have cried when I sketched those guys.... This was a tragic time; yet the people survived."

Hutchinson couldn't help them, but he could create memorable sketches of his friends and neighbours that would keep their woeful lives during the Depression remembered for generations.

His art was an attempt, he claimed, to "make a record of the terrible injustice that was thrust upon these people." Hutchinson had switched from painting to printmaking during the 1920s, so that his art would be more affordable for working people.

In the Depression, his work was considered political commentary. The establishment preferred to forget what Hutchinson sketched. "I was called an agitator, bolshevik, Communist, Marxist — everything under the sun." Yet Hutchinson persisted. "Wherever people worked, I'd be there. That was my slogan." In the workplaces, meeting halls and festive sites where working people gathered, he saw "the bravery of them —

they had the spirit in them that you couldn't kill... I enjoyed it. I fought back all the time, you see, because it needed people to fight, because the people were getting very dejected and afraid of fighting because of the authorities."

The stonecutter-turned-politician, Sam Lawrence, had the most impact on Hutchinson, after the influential painter Vincent Van Gogh.

As the labour movement's standout politician, alderman Sam Lawrence helped get Hutchinson appointed curator of the Hamilton Art Gallery in 1936. Art had a way of creating controversy, however. The Hamilton Art Assoication refused to display a Hutchinson woodcut showing a locked-out worker from Dominion Foundries and Steel. Lawrence reportedly told the affluent association members: "You hang him or I'll hang you!"

Hutchinson continued to make art serve the interests of ordinary people. He opened the first art classes for children at the gallery. He even opened the Art Gallery basement to vagrants.

An accomplished artist, elected as an associate of the Royal Canadian Academy in 1936, Hutchinson also identified with the broad heritage of art. As a Gallery curator, he bought many classical works, believing that these too were part of the people's heritage.

A labourer who appears in his print, "Protest", interrupted Hutchinson while he was sketching one day: "What are you going to do with us?" Hutchinson replied: "A hell of a lot."

Another Hamilton creative artist was Claudius Gregory, a printing company salesman who wrote novels as a sideline. His 1933 novel *Forgotten Men* is sentimental by today's literary standards. But the book captures the sense of crisis that people felt during the Depression.

The hero is portrayed as a Christ-like figure who is martyred by the authorities. Twelve "apostles" promise to carry on his work. Gregory wrote the novel in the belief that "the time has come when we can no longer leave the matter in the hands of the few, who through the power of tremendous holdings they cannot possibly use, created and must be held responsible for the unemployment and misery... that we call depression."

In the novel, Peter is an organizer. Addressing a crowd of unemployed, Peter exclaims: "There is plenty for everyone, yet we are not able to get even the bare necessities of life because we have no money to pay for them. We have no money because we are deprived of a chance to earn it because there is already too much of everything, and so on; a vicious circle...."

The hero, Christopher, tries his hand at charity work but quickly tires of its "patchwork methods... The fabric of civilization is too rotten to hold together. A patch might cover the rottenness, might hide it temporarily, but it would not endure." Christopher learns that "there is not and can never be an oversupply of any commodity until every living being in the entire world has what he needs..." He becomes leader of the Society of Forgotten Men and proposes solutions to the Depression such as inheritance taxes, limits on the size of corporations, and public ownership of large enterprises.

In 1937, Gregory took a job as editor of the *Dofasco Illustrated News*, the company paper. While at Dofasco, he convinced management to replace its semi-professional varsity sports teams with intramural leagues which allowed more participation by ordinary workers.

# Imagine . . .

The Depression was a devastating experience. Millions of people saw their dreams destroyed by forces they could not control or understand. Some never recovered their faith.

Others tried to build a new world out of dreams. "Imagine," invited a reporter from the Hamilton *Herald*, "a small community somewhere near Hamilton, where 20, 50 or perhaps 100 families live in perfect harmony. Where unemployment is just another forgotten bogey. Where men...work...happily at vocations they enjoy and where children grow up healthy and happy."

Such was the vision of ten men and twenty women at Hamilton's Dale Community Centre. Meeting and working in the Salvation Army hall on Concession Street, they laid plans for a new kind of community.

"What we need," explained the chairman of the Centre, John Stringer, "is a tract of land, not necessarily a farm, close enough to a large centre, to provide a suitable market for our produce." He hoped for "five or ten families in the first year... each with separate residences centred around a community hall housing various workshops."Members would grow their own food. They would earn money for other necessities by selling the products of their workshops.

Help to get started came from the Family Service Bureau of Hamilton. Women took classes in sewing, knitting, home nursing and nutrition. The men learned carpentry, metal working and weaving. Fred Flatman, the labour activist and lifelong socialist, taught metal working. Before long, Flatman attracted an unemployed iron welder. Together they formed the "Oriental Hand-Wrought Studio." That year, they sent out Christmas cards expressing the hope that "as darkest shadows yawn before brightest glare, may the coming year bring light and contentment to you, yours and mankind."

Social workers from the Family Service Bureau watched over the members and the activities of the centre. A carpenter nicknamed "Priddy" was described in one report as giving "the impression of being dull... but has the wit of the typical East Ender" in Cockney London. Another man, from St. Gall in Switzerland, "has successfully managed to retain some ownership in a cow in spite of regulations ... He has fixed notions that children must be brought up on a lot of cow's milk."

William Patterson, the report continued, "is interesting because of his Communistic views. He does not mix well and has to be leader or nothing." Yet, Patterson attracted more than 100 people to his Sunday evening forums at the Markeen Gardens.

Members of the Dale Community Centre failed to establish their utopian dream of a New Man in a New Society. Dreams were not enough. A hostile system still in awe of money and profit did not permit utopian socialism in its midst.

In 1938, some members at the centre chose a new course. Joining hands with labour organizations from across the city, they marched in the May Day rally. Political isolation had changed to political commitment. The community disbanded, but its members' faith in the potentially infinite humanity of work and workers remained. They expressed their ideals in the John Masefield poem "Fragments," which hung in their hall:

*But at the falling of the tide*
*The golden birds still sing and gleam,*
*The Atlanteans have not died*
*Immortal things still give us dream.*

*The dream that fire's man's heart to make,*
*To build, to do, to sing or say,*
*A beauty death can never take,*
*An Adam from the crumbled clay.*

# The Right to Live

"One cold September night in 1935," remembered Alex McLennan, a group of Hamilton men entered a public washroom. They "were shocked to encounter a group of about thirty unemployed transient workers who had made their bed for the night on newspapers laid out on the floor of the toilet." The newcomers persuaded the transients to at least try the city hostel or "flophouse." But the flophouse had its rules: No Vacancy for transients.

Moving on, the aroused transients woke up the Provincial Minister of Welfare, who threatened them with accommodation in the city jail. Another night visitation, this time to Reverend Banks Nelson, finally pressured the mayor into opening the city hostel. The next day, determined not to be shuffled around any more, the men formed the Association of Transient Unemployed. "The Right To Live" became their slogan.

These men were not alone in their struggles. Thousands of Canadians took direct action to improve their conditions. They saw no other way. Labour representatives like J.S. Woodsworth and A.A. Heaps highlighted their plight in Parliament. But Prime Minister R.B. Bennett offered nothing. People had to build something themselves.

In Hamilton, protests of the unemployed began in the winter of 1930. William Patterson, recently arrived from Glasgow, Scotland, was among the first to raise his voice. "We, the unemployed," he declared, "must demonstrate that we are not going to starve under park benches or incline railways quietly."

A month later, the Hamilton *Spectator* reported on a demonstration that "climaxed weeks of unrest" among the jobless. The protest began in the morning at the John Street Haymarket. After "impassioned speeches" that "stirred the mob to a pitch of excitement," the crowd moved "like a wave" north on John Street to Jackson, where the police, some on horseback, made several arrests. After the arrests, the crowd rushed to the police station "where they stood quiet in defiant groups, while practically the whole of the Hamilton police formed a cordon around the station building."

Two years later, an even larger group joined the May Day Rally at Woodlands Park. May Day rallies, commemorating the struggle of workers for the eight-hour day, had always drawn big crowds in Hamilton. Thousands turned out in 1932. Instead of the speeches they came to hear, the crowd saw a battle between police and demonstrators that climaxed when specially-deputized firemen burst from the Hamilton Arena and turned fire hoses on the people. For Johnny Greig, then working in his brothers' neighbourhood variety store, the actions of the firemen "created more Communists than you could shake a stick at."

By 1934, the momentum for a national chain of protest was building. In an effort to cool the growing anger, authorities everywhere imposed virtual martial law. They banned picketing and public meetings. In Hamilton, civic authorities passed a by-law ordering an end to public rallies of workers. Aimed principally at the Communist Party, which was commonly blamed for all unrest, the new by-law failed to contain radical organizing among the unemployed. The Workmen's Protective Association carried petitions on the right to free speech. A delegation of 150 men and women upset city hall routine with demands for an increase in relief, better food, a free monthly haircut and later hours in the flophouse.

Six weeks later, in January 1935, unrest broke out again when many of the city's relief workers stopped work to protest their conditions. Welfare Commissioner Kappelle sent letters to the families of the relief strikers, threatening to cut off their relief altogether. "Steps will be taken," he warned, "to prosecute as vagrants all those refusing to mention their families when offered work." The strikers reluctantly gave up.

At times, the efforts of the unemployed received militant support: Peter Hunter, a member of the junior section of the Hamilton ILP, remembered confronting the bailiff at the doors of families facing eviction. If the bailiff could not be persuaded to stop, "a volunteer corps would return the furniture as fast as it came out." Furniture piled on the streets was decorated with the picture of a British bulldog "standing over a draped Union Jack with the slogan below, 'What We Have, We'll Hold'."

Organizers of the unemployed met defeat more often than victory. Nevertheless they made more than one longstanding contribution to the Canadian working class movement. They helped win the right to demonstrate, a cornerstone of modern civil liberties. As well, they helped train many of the men and women who later emerged as stalwarts in the movement toward a new unionism.

# Changes

The Depression demanded change — change in the way people thought, the way governments acted and the way workers organized. By the mid 1930s, change was in the air. Prime Minister R.B. Bennett introduced his "little New Deal." It was too little, too late. Canadians ousted him from office and returned his opponent, Mackenzie King.

The structure of unionism had to change too. For too long, union organizers had watched as isolated groups of skilled tradesmen fell before the power of their employers.

Sheet mill workers at Stelco were among the first to press for these changes. They had been organized since 1919, only one year after Stelco introduced its two hand-powered sheet mills. To run their new machines, the company brought in skilled men from the United States. These men brought along their union, the Amalgamated Association of Iron, Steel and Tin Workers. By 1920, the Hamilton lodge was strong enough to win company agreement on the union's proposed sliding scale of wages, tied to such factors as the market price for steel and the quantity of output.

Thus, union members kept a close watch on the price of steel and rewrote the wage contract every day if necessary.

Prolonged and formal negotiations were not part of the union's style. Instead, whenever price increases did not register with take home pay, the company faced determined on-the-job action. "Tongs were banged," recounted veteran sheet mill unionist Tom McClure. "The whistle blown the mill stopped rolling, the men marched to the office, and as a general rule the appropriate changes were made...."

However, membership in the Amalgamated waned during the 1920s. By the early 1930s, the Steel Company felt free to dispense with the sliding scale without even notifying the men. Wages were cut by 33% between 1929 and 1933.

As resentment increased, the sheet mill workers began exploring their options. Some called for affiliation with the Communist Party's Sheet and Metal Workers Industrial Union. Others favoured the old Amalgamated. Both sides compromised on an Independent Steelworkers Union. In 1935, the union sent a committee to interview the superintendent about a new scale.

Nine months later, the men were still waiting. Stelco President Ross McMaster added to the tension by announcing plans to build a new strip mill. The new mill, McMaster boasted, would produce sheet steel in continuous strips and require only 75 men, "replacing the 250 necessary on the old mill." Worried now about jobs as well as pay, 300 men walked out.

It was a daring act to strike one of Canada's largest corporations in the midst of the Depression, especially when President McMaster warned that "beyond a certain date those who do not return to work will be regarded as having severed their connection with the company." Yet every man held firm. They knew, the *Herald* reported, "that there are no other sheet mills in Canada and that therefore there are few men here skilled in their kind of work."

Support for the strikers came from trade unions throughout the city. Sam Lawrence, Hamilton's CCF member of the Ontario Legislature, spoke to a "Solidarity and Organization" rally. A women's auxiliary of "wives and sweethearts" joined the fray, backing their loved ones who returned from work "fatigued to the extent that the children would have to be restricted in order that their fathers could rest."

It was a fight, one leader realized, "not only in our interests, but for unionism as a whole." Yet, after ten days on the line, the men accepted a company offer which granted a wage increase but refused to implement the Amalgamated scale or recognize the union.

The men were disappointed with these mixed results but determined to fight again. "We quit," recalled Tom McClure, "with the idea that we would be more likely to obtain our objectives if the whole plant was organized." What was needed, reasoned the union's paper *The Steel Workers News*, was "one industrial union," strong enough to "carry on the fight of the workers against unfair exploitation, to maintain an adequate wage scale, proper hours of work and rest, and to strive for unity among all steel-workers irrespective of nationality, colour, creed or the importance of their particular job as a steelworker." Shortly after the strike, the men applied for a charter as an industrial union.

The structure of unionism at Stelco had changed. Skilled and unskilled workers could now belong to a single organization. In 1936, it gained new strength by affiliating with the Committee for Industrial Organization and its Steel Workers Organizing Committee. Stelco unionists received their charter, and Lodge 1005 was born.

The strike of Stelco sheet mill workers was a turning point in the development of unionism in Hamilton. Although a formal contract eluded them for many years to come, the core of union men who survived the strike stuck to their cause with ingenuity and commitment. They helped industrial unionism take root in Hamilton.

# Labour's Civil War

The spectacular success of the union militance that was winning victories across the United States in the mid-1930s was clear for all to see. Even school kids began imitating the tactics that won fame in U.S. auto plants. One class of Hamilton grade 8 students petitioned their teacher for permission to stand and look out the window. In retaliation, the teacher ordered a "ringleader" to remain standing. The student grew tired and sat down. "Standup strike ends in sitdown," mused the *Spectator* headline of March 8, 1937.

For month after month, the victories of U.S. auto and steelworkers stole the headlines. Steel was the first target of the newly-formed Committee for Industrial Organization. Over $500,000 was placed at the disposal of Phillip Murray, acting director of the Steel Workers Organizing Committee. SWOC made its breakthrough at United States Steel, the largest steel producer in the U.S. The C.I.O. could not be stopped.

In Canada, the drive for industrial organization stalled. A spontaneous strike of Oshawa autoworkers in 1937 gained massive community support, yet barely withstood the frenzy of hysteria unleashed by Premier Mitchell Hepburn. The strike ended without recognition of the U.A.W. In the same year, a largely immigrant workforce occupied the Holmes Foundry near Sarnia. The strikers were terrorized and defeated by anti-union mobs.

The *Spectator* supported Hepburn and lashed out at the new tactics such as sit-down strikes. "The introduction of this alien method is contrary to all the honourable principles by which organized labour on this continent has achieved its progress," the paper lectured. But "honourable principles" only guaranteed strike-bound employees the right to bring in strikebreakers under police escort. There was no equivalent to the Wagner Act in Canada, no guarantee of the right to form a union and have it recognized. Canadian workers waited until World War II for these reforms.

Hamilton glassworkers fell victim to Canada's inadequate labour legislation when they battled the Dominion Glass Company in 1936. Striking for union recognition and wage increases, the company's moulders and machinists belatedly welcomed the unskilled plant workers to their picket lines. Although 700 men walked the picket lines, management broke the strike by bringing in strikebreakers under police escort.

Former glassworker Steve Dwyer recalls that it was "pretty rough on the picket line." The police were "down there in droves... protecting the company, not protecting the workers." The trucks crossing the line were just a provocation, he claimed. "For what they ship in, you could put in your eye."

While labour took its lumps on the picket lines in Hamilton, friction between craft and industrial unions increased. Nothing could prevent the importation of the fierce hatred between craft and industrial unionists in the United States. Local labour council meetings regularly degenerated into shouting matches. Finally, in May 1937, with the industrial unionists in the majority, Ontario AFL organizer John Noble lifted the council's AFL charter. Quickly the industrial unionists — including steelworkers, stonecutters, cap makers, projectionists, milk drivers, bakery workers, pipefitters and electricians — formed a new council.

They continued to hold the charter of the Trades and Labour Congress.

Inter-union conflict extended to many areas. An embarrassing example found Local 10 of the National Union of Theatrical Employees picketing the Tivoli, Palace and Strand theatres, while members of the International Alliance of Theatrical Employees paced the sidewalk in front of the Granada Theatre where a Canadian union staffed the house.

Political differences as well, placed the old AFL-Trades and Labor Congress, and the up-start CIO at loggerheads. The craft unionists wanted no part of the alleged socialist and Communist politics of the CIO. They clung to the well-worn dictum of former AFL president Sam Gompers to "reward your friends and punish your enemies." The new council, with Sam Lawrence as president and steelworker

Harry Hunter as vice-president, scoffed at the crafts' neutrality which usually ended up in support of the Conservatives.

Lawrence and the CIO council understood the fragility of their new organization and tried to broaden their base. One new ally was the Rev. John T. Stapleton who preached unionism in a letter to the *Spectator*: "Are you satisfied with the working conditions and wages of this Province?" he asked. "If you are we can understand your opposition to labour's choice of industrial organization in preference to craft organization... If you are not satisfied, what are you doing about it now? For nine long years I have served as Minister in the industrial section of this city, and my soul cries out for a move forward by all progressively-minded people to make in Ontario a 'kingdom wherein dwelleth righteousness.'"

# The Dofasco Way

The writing was on the wall for any employer who cast his eyes on U.S. developments. Workers were turning to unions in all the mass production industries. Could employers break the momentum of this massive movement by eliminating some of the most blatant abuses of traditional management practices? Could they kill the independence and security of unionism with kindness?

Many employers thought so. As early as 1910, some Hamilton-area manufacturers had begun experimenting with various schemes of welfare capitalism. They offered pensions, picnics and even company unions as an antidote to the attraction of unionism. One Hamilton company honed these techniques to perfection in the 1930s.

Dominion Foundries and Steel, like many Hamilton employers, sensed the need to address the growing discontent among employees. The close contact between employer and employee was breaking down. President Frank Sherman "decided to go to the employees and ask them why."

In 1935, Sherman launched a suggestion contest and offered a new Ford Sedan for the best ideas. The suggestions informed management of two major concerns. Workers wanted retirement security and they wanted to know their employers better. The introduction of a new tin mill promised growth but created anxiety about greater distance between employers and employees. The Depression heightened fears of an impoverished old age, on small pensions.

"We took these suggestions seriously," said Sherman, "and immediately started annual picnics, annual Christmas parties, and strengthened our personnel department." But nothing changed in the factory itself. "It was the dirtiest place in the world," one foundry worker recalled. "Dust lay everywhere. Fumes from the electric furnaces and core ovens filled the building." The noise from the finishing department where the castings were cleaned, "would blow your brains out."

Harsh conditions and low wages were fertile ground for union organizers. Foundry workers were the most receptive. Primarily eastern and southern Europeans, many became charter members of Local 1004 of the Steel Workers Organizing Committee.

Hopes ran high that a quick victory at Dominion Foundries would throw open the door to industrial unionism for all of Hamilton's iron and steelworkers. Dofasco management moved quickly. Union organizers were dismissed or laid off.

Employees attending street corner meetings or selling the union newspaper were placed under continual surveillance by company officials.

Claudius Gregory, a Hamilton-area author, was hired to start a company magazine to explain the mutual concerns of management and employees. A senior employee, David Richardson, took on what the *Dofasco Illustrated News* described as "the biggest job any man could hope to have" — "bringing contentment and trust and loyalty to the hearts of many hundreds of men who make up the Dominion Foundries and Steel Organization."

Another management official viewed these developments less innocently. "There was nothing in the world they wanted more," he believed, "than to keep the union out. That is what they were fighting all the time. The union was a cancer to them."

In May, 1938, Dofasco introduced strong medicine to cure the "cancer." It was profit-sharing. Workers with three years continuous service could invest up to $120 in the "Fund." The company would match this money four-fold by contributing at least 10% of net profits to the

"Fund." The "Employee Savings and Profit Sharing Fund," the *Illustrated News* proclaimed, "should set a new standard of understanding and coopera-tion between Labour and Capital, giving the worker increased opportunity for improving his position in life and of winning for himself a measure of independence and security."

Some older workers of European descent were suspicious. They feared the company was taking money from them by some trick. The more skilled and highly paid workers greeted the Fund more enthusiastically. They could put more into it and receive a greater pension. Meanwhile, the Fund supplied the company with a new pool of capital for investment. Profit-sharing served every-one. It proved to be the cornerstone of the "Dofasco Way."

What unions would have to negotiate from the profits of reluctant employers, Dofasco seemed to be "giving" to its employees. Every worker had a personal motive to work harder, since each would receive more of the profits. This new management technique earned the praise of the *Illustrated News*; it symbolized a "spirit of comradeship which makes us

sincerely interested in each other's welfare."

This "spirit of comradeship" rang hollow to those workers dismissed for loyalty to the union rather than to Dofasco management. Likewise, the "open door" policy announced by the company, which allowed individual workers to take their complaints over the heads of foremen right to top management, had no provision for union committees. There was no independent, neutral grievance-solving procedure.

Paul Nykolyn, a retired Dofasco bricklayer, remembered how the 1945 union drive campaigned under the slogan "Let's have a union and let's have the Fund." The company retaliated with rumours of "union then no Fund." Mansfield Mathias, another one-time employee, remembered that "people were systematically fired soon after signing a union card," a clear indication of "at least one company spy on the organizing committee." There was, it seemed, little workaday independence to correspond with the retirement security of the "Dofasco Way."

Dominion Foundries workers receive statements of contributions to profit-sharing fund, 1938.

# A War for Democracy

From the production line to the firing line, Hamilton working people felt the full impact of World War II.

Hamilton's heavy industries boomed to meet the demands of a war economy. Industry strained at full capacity for the first time in a decade. Women and senior citizens poured into the industrial army as thousands of young workers joined up to fight Hitler — 1,300 from Stelco alone.

Productivity was the watchword. Tonnage records were scored almost daily. It was an ideal environment for employers. Their order books filled with military contracts . Expansion was financed with government subsidies and special depreciation allowances. Dofasco netted almost eight million dollars in such compensation by June, 1944.

The war also helped foster a climate of military unity and loyalty within the work force. War bond drives regularly went over the top. Management warned against union organizers breaking down such co-operation and good feelings. One Stelco vice-president felt secure with "war veterans scattered throughout the plants." They provided, he was sure, a "steadying influence" and "protection against subversive elements and possible sabotage."

Workers, however, gradually began to take a different view. Steady work and regular pay broke down the anxieties and lack of confidence wrought by years of depression. Wartime regulations made it difficult to dismiss workers, and union activists strode defiantly through the plants. Returning soldiers took the fight for democracy to the workplace. Bill Scandlan, an employee at Stelco's Canada Works, was typical. He refused to conceal his union sympathies. "Hell," he exclaimed, "what kind of democracy is this when you are being subjected to the very thing they were sending the boys over there to fight."

By 1943, with Hitler on the run, Hamilton workers began to look ahead to the post-war era. The fight for industrial democracy fused with the demand for social security. Unemployment insurance had been introduced two years earlier. But it was not enough. "Social security," wrote government advisor Leonard Marsh, "has become one of the things for which the peoples of the world are fighting. It is one of the concrete expressions of 'a better world' which is particularly real to those who knew unemployment, destitution, inadequate medical care and the like in the depression periods before the war."

Workers would have to fight for their security. Employers opposed demands for social legislation and industrial democracy, but a rising tide of industrial militancy swept aside their resistance. Unions pressed for favourable collective bargaining legislation, arguing that this was needed to equalize the wartime freeze on wages and the ban on free movement from job to job. If workers were regulated, then the practices of industry must be regulated to ensure the right to collective bargaining, unionists insisted. Unions got an assist when the Ontario legislature passed the Collective Bargaining Act in the spring of 1943. Labour pressure also brought about the passage of Privy Council Order P.C. 1003 in February, 1944. As a result, Canadian workers were free to organize in unions of their choosing. If unions won majority support, employers had to bargain with them.

Hamilton employers had been in the forefront of business opposition to these new bargaining laws. A petition bearing the signatures of every major employer charged the legislation with providing "a rallying point for dissident and malcontent minority groups seeking to secure sole and exclusive rights by biased and well-known means, such as biased voting, closed shop, etc."

When the war was over, many of Hamilton's industries were unionized. The armies of the production line and the firing line joined together to crack the anti-union armour of the city's heavy industries. "Coming back from the war after seeing the tyranny of the Hitler people," recalled former steelworker Jake Isbister, "I thought to myself: I don't want to live under any kind of tyranny where a company is the sole arbitrator in anything you might want to say. I felt there was a need for some kind of representation by the men themselves." The people, it seemed, agreed.

# Three Strikes and Out

When war was declared, union leaders pledged the full co-operation of labour. But "such co-operation did not mean passive acquiescence to the interpretations placed upon government regulations by the employer," cautioned Murray Cotterill of the Steel Workers Organizing Committee. "It means that labour accepts sacrifices, when it has an equal say to its government and employer partners in drawing up conditions which make such sacrifices necessary."

National Steel Car had no intention of giving its workers an equal say. In February 1941, union sympathizers were dismissed — among them George Tanner, president of the local. SWOC took the company to court.

Court proceedings failed to relieve the tensions. Steel Car officials refused to reinstate the discharged employees, especially Tanner. A full page *Globe & Mail* advertisement informed readers that to reinstate him "would be resented by a great body of our highly competent production and supervisory staff."

The firm offered to reinstate two of the employees if the union would withdraw its request for a conciliation board under Mackenzie King's Industrial Disputes Investigation Act. The union refused. The eyes of basic steelworkers across Canada were on Hamilton, proclaimed SWOC National Director, Charlie Millard. "They want to know if the Industrial Disputes Act is going to be flouted indiscriminately or whether they are going to receive a measure of protection."

Conflicts on the shopfloor increased the need for union protection. John Dowling, a steward, replied to the *Globe* advertisement with a letter outlining the speed-ups and wage-cutting practices of the company. The men had to turn out 9,000 shells in the same time as they had previously produced 2,500, Dowling claimed. Upon reaching the new quota, "the operators were astounded that their piece rates were cut 33 per cent, which caused a complete work stoppage and an explanation stating, 'That's the new price, boys. Take it or leave it. There are men outside the gates to take your jobs, so if you want to make your usual day's wages, give us more shells'."

The breaking point came when 18 men had their rates cut below those of their helpers. "The men had taken their last licking — they went out," Dowling explained. "A sudden alarm arose in the plant. Men began to stand on their feet, and when the morning shift arrived all operators ceased to work in sympathy with their fellow workers. A feeling of unity arose and the men organized."

"A Strike For Industrial Democracy," one picket sign blazed. Others demanded Tanner's reinstatement and the right to a plant vote on unionization. Steelworkers at Algoma Steel in Sault Ste. Marie telegrammed their readiness to strike in sympathy.

In response, the federal government placed the company under trusteeship. Confident that the government controller would negotiate with them, the men returned to work. Disappointment set in quickly when a 1,740 to 542 vote in favour of the union brought no action from the controller, E.J. Brunning. His replacement by a new controller led only to further stalling. A July 28 meeting in the Winter Gardens sent union workers back to the picket lines.

That evening, the first pickets were attacked and beaten by soldiers from the Army Trades School on Ottawa Street. Defence Minister J.R. Ralston refused any comment on the actions of his soldiers. Mayor William Morrison only criticized the strikers for harassing those trying to work. The next night, a reinforced picket line was flanked by military police on all roads leading to the plant. As darkness fell over the National Steel Car plant, it resembled an armed camp.

New government promises led to a return to work four days later. No action meant another walkout, warned Millard. Mackenzie King installed a third controller. C.D. Howe, Minister of Munitions and Supply, took a harder line and stated flatly that no union had exclusive bargaining rights. "It is a case of three strikes and out," he ruled.

Howe would prevail. The steelworkers failed to establish their union. Still, their confrontation with one of the city's most bitter anti-union employers raised the issue of union recognition to the forefront of public debate. Unlike their American counterparts, Canadian unionists could not grant a no-strike pledge. The hostility of employers like National Steel Car and the inactivity of the Canadian government confirmed the necessity of strike action. Kirkland Lake miners learned the same lesson in their strike in 1941-2. Together, National Steel Car workers in Hamilton and miners in Kirkland Lake helped force federal and provincial governments to introduce legislation requiring employers to recognize the unions demanded by their workers.

The men were disappointed with these mixed results but determined to fight again. "We quit," recalled Tom McClure, "with the idea that we would be more likely to obtain our objectives if the whole plant was organized." What was needed, reasoned the union's paper *The Steel Workers News*, was "one industrial union," strong enough to "carry on the fight of the workers against unfair exploitation, to maintain an adequate wage scale, proper hours of work and rest, and to strive for unity among all steelworkers irrespective of nationality, colour, creed or the importance of their particular job as a steelworker." Shortly after the strike, the men applied for a charter as an industrial union.

The structure of unionism at Stelco had changed. Skilled and unskilled workers could now belong to a single organization. In 1936, it gained new strength by affiliating with the Committee for Industrial Organization and its Steel Workers Organizing Committee. Stelco unionists received their charter, and Lodge 1005 was born.

The strike of Stelco sheet mill workers was a turning point in the development of unionism in Hamilton. Although a formal contract eluded them for many years to come, the core of union men who survived the strike stuck to their cause with ingenuity and commitment. They helped industrial unionism take root in Hamilton.

# The Moral is Simple

Hamilton employers honestly believed they could defeat trade unionism. Few tried harder than Stelco.

Directly after the 1935 sheet mill strike, Stelco introduced an "Employee Representation Plan" — a company union. The intention, according to President Ross McMaster's letter to each employee, was "the establishment of a definite and natural means by which the employees may discuss with the management any question affecting their welfare, working conditions, etc."

Union activists were not fooled, as these lines of sheet mill poet "Woodyard Coupling" indicated.

*The workers, making steel, have lately come*
*    to feel*
*The time has come when they should all*
*    unite*
*The bosses see it, too, and so, for me and*
*    you*
*They set up "Company Unions" left and*
*    right.*

*If their history we read, the lesson there*
*    we heed*
*Men don't fall for Company Unions when*
*    they're "wise"*
*But as soon as they are shown, join Unions*
*    of their own*
*Now the moral is so simple – ORGANIZE!*

The poem was published in the first issue of the *Steel Workers News*, and handed out at the plant gates in September 1935.

Arguments by union supporters that this works council would be "completely under company control" failed to convince. A majority of Stelco workers voted to support the Plan. Not to be denied, union activists like Milton Montgomery and Tom McClure won elections to the works council. There, under full view of management and workers alike, they regularly took up issues of higher wages and paid holidays.

Just as regularly, the company refused to consider these issues. Employees, Stelco claimed, were receiving their fair share. Instead, management representatives turned the discussion to bus routes, bicycle paths, safety, company sports, and the benefits of the Stelco insurance and pension plans.

Yet concessions were won. Bi-annual and then quarterly bonuses took the place of wage increases. In 1938, employees with 10 to 25 years of service were granted one week's vacation with pay; those with more service received two weeks. The works council also got the company to agree to follow seniority in the event of lay-offs. At times, the council functioned as a virtual grievance committee, with special meetings called to consider rehiring discharged employees.

At first, the war made organizing more difficult. New workers replaced union stalwarts who went off to fight. The War Measures Act froze wartime incomes and undermined one of the union's most potent organizing issues.

Still, by 1942 the union felt strong enough to flex its muscles. Eight union candidates stood for the eight employee seats on a new works council. All were elected. Soon after, in January 1943, steelworkers at Sydney and Sault Ste. Marie went out on strike. Tom McClure rose to address the first meeting of the new works council: "We are against a strike, but this is a crisis," said McClure. "The matter can be solved... if the company will sit with us to discuss ways and means of arriving at a collective bargaining agency. I move that the works council recommend to the management that the company be a party with the union to apply for an immediate vote to determine a collective bargaining agency and agree to abide by the vote."

The management representatives on the works council were opposed, and Stelco President McMaster broke the tie vote to defeat union recognition. Nine employee representatives walked out. The proceedings of the works council came to an abrupt halt. Management tried to revive its much-troubled council by asking defeated candidates to replace those who had resigned. All but two complied. Unionists had a field day, ridiculing these unelected stand-ins as a "bob-tailed council of minority representatives."

"NOW IS THE TIME," exhorted one SWOC bulletin, "when every individual must decide whether he is for democracy or dictatorship — whether he supports the right of working men and women to choose how they will be represented or whether he supports 'der fuehrer' policy of having the bosses say how workers may present their cause."

Lacking in credibility, the works council lapsed into silent death a few months later. Its ashes were still warm when a company-inspired Independent Steelworkers Association sprang up in its place. According to its officers, the Association had a "Provincial Charter giving it the right on behalf of employees of the Steel Company of Canada... to look after their interests socially, economically, and in regards to Employer-Employee relations."

But organizing for a real union continued. PC 1003 paved the way for union certification after a government supervision of votes. Some 4,463 Stelco workers were eligible to vote. In February, 1944, the United Steelworkers of America swamped the Association — 2,461 to 889. The tide had turned. "Company Unionism" was in the past. Now, could they get a contract?

# Something to Crow About

The earth-shaking events of World War II tilted the axis of Canadian politics permanently to the left. Even the do-nothing "laissez faire" leaders of the old-line parties had no choice but to retreat before the groundswell of popular determination to never again suffer the despair of depression.

The first shock came in February, 1942, when unknown CCF candidate Joseph Noseworthy stunned the nation by defeating arch-Tory Arthur Meighen's bid for a political comeback in a Toronto by-election. Dazed, the unsettled Conservatives hastily prefixed "Progressive" to their name and laced social security measures into their electioneering.

Mackenzie King and the Liberals kept their ears to the ground a little longer. They were forced to move when two CCF by-election victories in August 1943 and a September Gallup Poll showed that the CCF could trample over both Liberals and Conservatives. In Ontario, the discredited Liberal regime, hard-pressed by both Conservatives and the CCF, tried to salvage its reputation by passing legislation which enabled collective bargaining. King followed suit in 1944, passed P.C. 1003 which established ground rules for unionization of war industries, and carried through with other social welfare measures such as the "baby bonus."

The CCF, the party which set the tempo for all these motions toward change, had come a long way since its founding in 1933. Its Regina Manifesto promised that "No CCF government will rest content until it has eradicated capitalism and put into operation the full program of socialized planning that will lead to the establishment in Canada of the Co-operative Commonwealth."

The first test came in the 1934 Ontario provincial elections. Running in Hamilton East, popular alderman Sam Lawrence was the only successful CCF candidate. His victory heightened the suspicions of old Independent Labor Party members who opposed the CCF's commitment to complete political independence and socialism. The divisions widened in the 1935 federal election, when the CCF ran John Mitchell against Independent Labor incumbent, Humphrey Mitchell. The labour vote was split, and allowed a Tory to take a triumphant run through the middle. There was, the *Spectator* pointed out, "bitter strife in the ranks of East Hamilton labor."

The CCF grew slowly. Lawrence was turned out of office in 1937. Later that year he returned to City Council as

Controller, but the victory was bitter-sweet. "It was a losing battle for many, many years," recalled former organizer Robert Harkness. "You never got anywhere. You got a door slammed in your face. You were told to 'get the hell out of here, you Red!'"

Suddenly, in 1943, there was a staggering breakthrough. Ontario voters sent 34 socialists to the legislature, including a full slate from Hamilton. Herbert O'Conner, an International Harvester employee, topped the polls in Hamilton East. A milk salesman, Robert Thornberry, championed the CCF cause in Hamilton Centre. An architect, Fred Warren, and a National Steel Car employee, William Robertson, won in Hamilton West and Hamilton Wentworth.

"I don't know what caused it," reflected William Robertson's brother, Dave. "When this election came along, honest to Jesus, we were really amazed. People were coming in to ask what they could do." Robert Harkness remembered what it was like "down at the plant. Oh everything, CCF! You got to vote CCF." When the four members were elected, "it was the first time we really had anything to crow about." For Sam Lawrence, the surge of the CCF expressed "the resentment of the manner in which labour has been kicked around."

Inspired by the party's rising fortunes, the Hamilton CCF ran a full slate for the municipal elections. Heading the list was mayoralty candidate Sam Lawrence. The *Spectator* was horrified. Daily editorials ranted against a "political doctrine that is Communist in concept, and would be Nazi in application.... A totalitarian state, with a Sovietized and Nazified Canada, is the goal of these wreckers."

Lawrence replied for the CCF. Civic elections "are the cornerstone of democracy," he insisted, and "an excellent place for the citizen to give expression to his or her determination that never again shall Canada be a country with unemployed, idle factories, and wasting natural resources."

Lawrence was looking beyond the war — to reconstruction and planning for peace. On election day, he won handily in the industrial wards and beat his opponent by 1,700 votes. Working class wards 5 and 8 held firm and also returned CCF aldermen. Elsewhere, the CCF candidates were defeated. Although mayor-elect Lawrence had to lead a non-CCF council, events would soon show that his victory was decisive. Hamilton now had a mayor representing the shifting moods of its working class population.

# Seven Days a Week

Unionism was the human rights movement of the 1940s. It promised to replace the arbitrary and petty rules of paternalistic employers with the security, independence and joint rule-setting of what some called "industrial democracy."

Before the rise of unionism, employers alone made the rules which governed every detail of industrial life. At Hamilton's Westinghouse plant, notices listed 20 ways an employee could lose his job. Smoking, "except at specified times, in designated areas," was prohibited. "Loitering in toilets, rest room and auxiliary areas" would bring dismissal. So could "leaving your own department or Plant during working hours without reasonable cause or permission." Orders from foremen and superintendents had to be obeyed, and no employee was allowed to make "false or malicious statements concerning the operations of the Plant, its products or other employees." Of course, union activity could also bring on a pink slip. When the United Electrical Radio and Machine Workers (UE) first started to organize Westinghouse, employees themselves could not get involved. "It was too risky to expose workers from the plant," recalled Bert McClure, a building trades electrician active in these early efforts.

Nevertheless, a few employees like Alf Ready risked showing up at the Barton Street office building rented by the Steel Workers Organizing Committee and shared by the UE and other CIO unions. Ready and other members of the new Local 504 of the UE distributed leaflets and put out a shop paper called *Union Light*. "When you are organizing a union," Ready recalled, "you just don't call a meeting once a month. You are going at it every day, seven days a week."

The union got an early chance to test its strength when UE national director C.S. Jackson was arrested during a wartime round-up of Communist Party supporters. Calls for a one-day protest brought 1,000 Westinghouse workers into the streets on June 24, 1941.

As in other major industries, however, progress was slow. "I don't think we had 50 members by 1942," recounted Ready. The company laid off all the union's stewards and a Canadian Westinghouse Employees Association mysteriously appeared. Just as mysteriously, men with ten years' service were suddenly granted one week vacations. Those with over ten years got two weeks. Women received one week's paid holiday after only three years.

The Association claimed credit for these advances. But sentiment for the UE continued to grow and Westinghouse's company union suffered an early demise. Still the company refused to negotiate.

UE efforts to organize Sawyer Massey proved equally frustrating. As a confidential government report recognized, Sawyer Massey was under a great deal of pressure, "directly or indirectly, from other large companies who are resisting C.I.O. activity in Hamilton."

Try as they might, Hamilton employers failed to stem the rising nation-wide demand for collective bargaining. Finally, in February 1944, Order in Council P.C. 1003 became law. Employers were forced to bargain with unions certified as having majority support.

P.C. 1003 gave new openings for union organizers across Hamilton. Workers at Firestone, who had already staged a sit-down and two-day walkout in 1943, won complete control of the company's "Conference Committee" in 1944. They promptly replaced it with the United Rubber Workers union. A government-supervised vote gave the real union a 962-177 victory. At Westinghouse, the results of the 1944 certification vote were overwhelmingly in favour of the union. Steelworkers won decisively at Stelco. Like the glaciers that scooped out Hamilton Bay in the Great Lakes, the movement for industrial democracy had edged forward imperceptibly but unmistakably. And nothing could stop it.

# Now that the War is Over

Business leaders grudgingly accepted government regulation over the wartime economy. When the war was over, their call for a return to the "free market" grew increasingly strident. The first signs of a developing confrontation were felt on the shop floor. Superintendents and foremen, their power and authority diminished by wartime regulations, waited impatiently for a return to the days of unchallenged control.

Canadian workers did not share such fond memories of pre-war times. The war years had brought a new sense of dignity and confidence, and they wanted to maintain the inroads made against management authority. They were worried about the pressing problems of post-war reconstruction. Many remembered the years of unemployment and hardship that followed World War I, when the government made few preparations and showed little concern.

The struggles for greater industrial and political democracy were joined first in Windsor. On September 12, 1945, over 10,000 autoworkers struck the Ford Motor Company of Canada.

Security was the central issue of the strike: security for the individual worker and for the union — the United Automobile Workers. Management had refused to meet employee demands for a "union shop," where all employees who benefitted from the contract would pay dues and belong to the union. The union held firm, arguing that compulsory union membership was the only safeguard against financial instability and management persecution of workers who signed for voluntary checkoff of dues. In a dramatic display of community solidarity, Windsor citizens abandoned their cars in the streets to blockade the factory and prevent police from re-opening the power plant.

The Ford strike ended with a compromise. Union and management accepted the conciliation report of Justice Ivan C. Rand. In place of the union shop, Rand granted the automatic check-off of union dues from all employees eligible for union membership. The "Rand Formula," as it became popularly known, proved to be a mixed blessing for autoworkers and unions, since severe fines and penalties awaited unions that struck outside the contract. Nevertheless, most workers viewed it as a step forward in securing the stability of their union.

Hamilton workers were among the strongest supporters of the Ford strikers. The day after the strike began, the CIO's Hamilton labour council authorized a motorcade to support the UAW. Council sent a telegram to labour minister, Humphrey Mitchell, and placed full blame for the strike on the government's failure to enact a national labour code with union protection.

Even Hamilton's craft unionists felt the urgency of the situation. They had already joined with industrial unionists in a September rally calling on the government to enact a 40 hour work-week to ease unemployment during post-war "reconversion." Unity prevailed over factionalism during the Ford strike. "It not only affects the C.I.O.," explained one delegate to the Hamilton Trades and Labor Council, "but all labor in Canada and if labor loses it will be a big blow to labor."

The union and job security goals of the Ford strikers touched all Hamilton workers. Tony Gervasio, a Stelco employee, came to understand the link between union and personal security when he was demoted from his foreman's job after Italy entered the war. Though a Canadian citizen, he was born of Italian parents. The demotion left him "very bitter," and he resolved to "go in and beat it." He joined the navy and returned a changed man. "I felt we were fighting for a better Canada and I felt when I came back home I could almost demand. A serviceman in 1945 was looked up to. I got a little stronger in union affairs. I was very bitter about losing my job and that's the biggest reason I became a staunch union man." With memories and expectations like these, thousands of others prepared for the new battle lines set to emerge in 1946.

Politics made its way to the workplace, Stelco 1945.

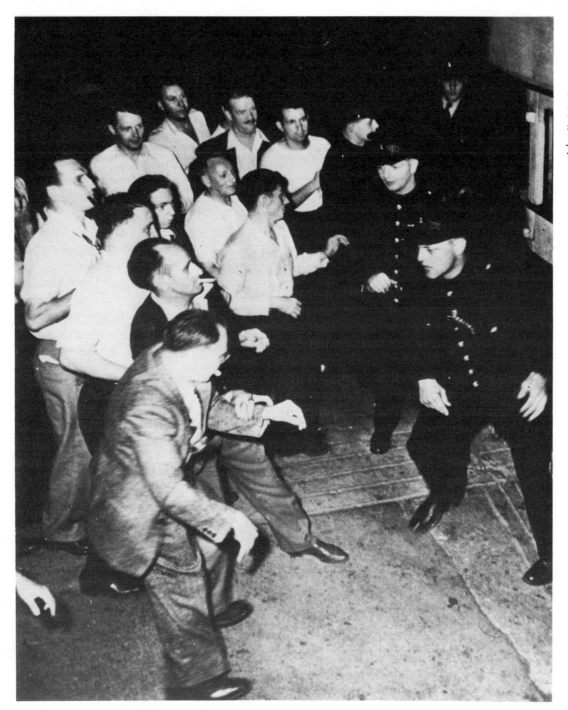

Unionists and police squaring off outside the Hamilton *Spectator* in 1946. Those on the union side included David Archer, George Harris, C.S. Jackson and "Shaky" Robertson.

# Conquering our Fears

"Having to take on (Stelco boss) Hugh Hilton in 1946 was like taking on the King," claimed Stew Cooke, a regional director of the Steelworkers who cut his union teeth in the Hamilton labour movement of the 1940s.

In 1946, the working people of Hamilton dethroned the city's industrial kings and barons and brought the era of the divine rights of employers to an end. Mayor Sam Lawrence understood the scale on which this achievement would be measured. He also understood the importance attached to victory by people who had just finished fighting a war against Hitler. "In the totalitarian nations the first objective of fascist rule has been the crushing of free trade unionism," he reminded one audience. "We in Canada should learn from the history of these countries that the preservation and strengthening of our unions is essential to the furthering of our democratic method.... We all have a stake in the program which labour has advanced for the future of industry in this city." The war for industrial democracy was on.

The atmosphere was charged with tension and high hopes when Hamilton's newly certified industrial unions sat down with company officials to iron out the first post-war contracts. From the outset,

all eyes turned to the negotiations in the basic steel industry, where the United Steelworkers of America had opted for industry-wide bargaining that united steelworkers in the fight for a common national settlement. Negotiations at Stelco in Hamilton, at Dosco in Sydney, Nova Scotia, and Algoma in Sault Ste. Marie were taken over by the union's National Advisory Committee (NAC).

The union modelled its demands on the "health and decency standard" set by the Welfare Council of Canada. Steel companies gravely undercut these standards. At the time of negotiations, Stelco employees worked a 48 hour week but still earned 19½ cents an hour below the decency standard for families. Workers had to wait 15 years for one week's paid vacation, and 25 years for two weeks. The union demanded $33.60 for a 40 hour work-week and two week paid vacations after five years. The unions also wanted an agreement along the lines of the compromise that settled the strike of Ford workers in Windsor. This settlement required all production workers to contribute dues toward the financial security of the union which fought on their behalf. This measure safeguarded both the financial security of the union and the individual security of the union member, since employers automatically "checked off" dues from each employee.

The steel companies rejected these demands wholesale. They held fast against any reduction in hours or any form of union check-off. They cut union wage demands in half, offering first five and then ten cent hourly increases.

The federal government cast a chilling eye on the union's wage demands and prohibited any thawing of the wartime wage-freeze. The government bias was clear for all to see, since it had just allowed a five dollar per ton hike in steel prices. The union rejected the government's Industrial Disputes Investigation Commission report (the Roach report) and set a strike deadline for July 15. On July 10, the government intervened again, this time to head off a strike. The cabinet imposed Order-in-Council P.C. 2901, slapped a trusteeship over the steel industry, and declared steel strikes illegal. Any unionist who dared to disobey faced fines and jail terms.

This only fuelled the anger of national steelworker leader Charles Millard, who rallied the membership for the fight of their lives. "No one should be fooled," he fumed. "The steel plants have not been seized by the government. The companies are still operating the mills, the companies are still getting the profits from their very profitable enterprise." P.C. 2901, he warned, "contains the fascist principle of forced labour. It violates the principles of British justice by judging the workers guilty until they have proven themselves innocent. It is a challenge to the democratic rights of citizens of Canada generally."

On July 14, a mass meeting of Stelco workers defied the government's challenge. The next day, 2,700 steelworkers went on strike. The "Battle of Stelco" was on.

The Stelco strikers were not alone. Far from it, they were latecomers in a city-wide movement that was taking on the proportions of a general strike. Hamilton Firestone workers were but one of 11 rubber worker locals in Ontario out on strike. They had been pounding the pavement since June 24, seeking an industry-wide settlement with 20 cent hourly increases and a 40 hour week. Electrical workers at Westinghouse had been out since July 8, demanding a 25 cent hourly wage hike and a 44 hour work week. Hundreds of representatives from these strikebound plants escorted the first Stelco pickets from a rally at the Playhouse Theatre to the Stelco gates.

Two days later, Mayor Lawrence led a parade of 10,000 strike supporters and unequivocally announced himself "a union man first and chief magistrate second." He assured the marchers that the "union program is not an extravagant or an impossible demand upon employers. It has the down-to-earth reasonableness that day to day experience in the plants has given to our Hamilton workers." If Stelco management had counted on public sympathy, they guessed wrong.

Stelco strikers needed all the support they could get, for the strike at Stelco was to be the acid test of industrial unionism in Canada. Only at Stelco, where the strength of the union remained suspect, did company officials decide to continue production. Indeed, weeks before the strike deadline, Stelco workers were ordered to build a landing strip to serve as a runway for company aircraft. Food supplies and beds were moved into the plant.

"Slag Mountain Lodge" became home for approximately 2000 men who spurned the strike call and were sealed inside the plant gates by union pickets. A special company paper, the *Stelco Billet* — "Rolled At The Hamilton Works By and For The Loyal Order of Scabs" — carried anti-union and anti-strike news from Hamilton and across North America.

The cause of the strikebreakers, all of whom were paid for 24 hour shifts in violation of Ontario and Canadian labour codes, was taken up by powerful political figures. At the federal level, acting Prime Minister Louis St. Laurent and his Minister of Labour, Humphrey Mitchell, expressed concern for the rights of strikebreakers to come and go as they pleased. Locally, Controller Nora Francis Henderson led the battle for extra police to crack down on picket lines and ensure law and order while people and goods entered the plants.

The Hamilton Police Commission, with Lawrence as one of its members, declined to call on outside police. Stymied by this refusal, Henderson moved that city council consult the Attorney General "as to the possible need to uphold law and order in the city of Hamilton." On August 8, city council debated her motion for two tumultuous hours. Outside city hall, an excited crowd of strike supporters serenaded council with the tune "We'll Hang Nora Frances By The Sour Apple Tree". Council rejected Henderson's motion.

Sympathy for the strikebreakers tried the patience of union steelworkers and drew the fire of the union paper, *Steel Labor*. Allowing Stelco to pay triple time to strikebreakers, the editor charged, "not only reveals Ottawa as a strikebreaker de luxe, but it negates the entire argument that higher wages are inflationary." The "strident shrieking" of Controller Henderson was particularly exasperating. She "may sound heroic to the voters she is trying to impress but to the thousands of strikers and their families now sacrificing for the sake of their futures, her mouthings are nauseating," the worked-up editor insisted. "Weeping crocodile tears about the poor, persecuted, triple pay scabs inside the steel mill may make good headlines but the sad lot of these pampered Judases will hardly cause any concern to any thinking Canadian."

It was a long, hot summer, but the crisis passed. When the spectre of a bloody clash between pickets and police filtered into the background, the strike settled into a war of attrition. A human barricade kept Stelco under siege, without supplies or sales. The union trenches surrounding the plant were bolstered by wives, families and friends who shared picket duty, helped prepare meals and took part-time jobs to keep the strikers solvent. Donations of food poured in from around the countryside. Financial aid arrived from unions and individual citizens, concerned that the workers not be forced to settle prematurely.

Steelworker Harry Pomeroy was amazed as he watched the contributions roll in. "I never knew that people could be rallied to a cause that wasn't their own. The degree of support we got was astronomical," he marvelled. "We had oodles and oodles of people that used to come down every night to the picket line to look around, talk to the boys and give them moral support. We had a collection box there, if they had a dime or a quarter. Some even dropped a dollar bill and in those days a dollar bill was a big thing."

World War II veterans donated their solidarity. Veterans were regulars at the picket line, especially when a delivery of supplies was in the offing. At one decisive juncture in the strike, The Hamilton Striking Veterans Committee organized a veterans' march to the Stelco gates. "Headed by a sound truck playing marching songs," the *Spectator* reported, they carried placards proclaiming "We vets are in the union army now." This march was credited with finally breaking the morale of Stelco management.

After two months of frantic activity, pressure began building for a settlement. It came first in steel. The government used Tom Rahilly, the president of Canada Cement, as a contact to get things moving toward a settlement. Rahilly knew that Stelco president Hugh Hilton suspected Millard's socialism and support for the C.C.F. Rahilly received Millard's assurances that he was a democratic socialist who did not expect to see socialism in his time, and then arranged a Montreal meeting with federal mediator F.B. Kilbourne. There, a telephone conversation between Millard and Hilton cleared the way for an agreement "in five minutes." According to Millard, Hilton agreed "that if in 15 days we could sign up a majority of the men with authorization for the check-off they would recognize our union and then they gave us 13 cents and allowed us to settle in good grace."

The proposed settlement was approved in a vote on September 28. On October 4, 81 days after the strike began, the picket lines came down. The actual signing of the contract was postponed until the following March, since Stelco refused to rehire men found guilty of criminal activity during the strike. The union wanted them all rehired. In the end, after the intervention of yet another federal mediator, Stelco agreed to reinstate 17 of the 24.

Westinghouse and Firestone workers settled a few weeks after Stelco. Once the fundamental precedents were set, bargaining in the other strikes was reduced to haggling over pennies along the pattern set by the Stelco contract.

Bill Walsh, a negotiator for the UE at Westinghouse, recalled how the gruff leader of the management team interrupted one unionist's humanitarian appeal and snapped: "You see, in this electrical industry, we have to buy many commodities. We have to buy copper, rubber. We have to buy steel. We buy mica, enamel, paint and many other commodities. When we buy these things, we pay the lowest price we possibly can." Then the manager let it all hang out. "We also need to buy your labour.... So let's talk about the price. We have to pay for the commodity you're going to sell us — your labour.... To us, labour is just like copper, rubber, steel, paint and so on. It's a commodity that we need. And we're going to buy it for the lowest price we can..."

For employers, the settlement of these strikes may have represented no more — and no less — than an obnoxious alternative to socialism. Thereafter, they would at least have to bargain over the price of their "labour commodities."

For the workers, the settlement of these strikes represented the culmination of a movement built on solidarity that was unparalleled in the city's history. Workers won their first real security, both in higher wages and in grievance systems which stripped away many of the dictatorial powers of company supervisors.

When Reg Gardiner looked back on his presidency of the Stelco local during the 1946 strike, it wasn't the pay increases or even the dues check-off that he remembered. More than 30 years later, he cherished the benefits "which could not be measured in dollars and cents." He still savoured the memories of that first day on the picket line. "I feel it yet. The feeling of freedom that we all felt by breaking the hold that Stelco had on us." Above all, he said, Hamilton workers had grown to "conquer our fears."

## A LABOR MAN FIRST

The strike was but two days old when 10,000 sympathizers paraded through the streets of Hamilton to demostrate their support. Mayor Sam Lawrence (wearing a suit and brim hat) marched in the front ranks and issued a ringing declaration that "I am a labor man first and chief magistrate second."

Three years earlier, in accepting the nomination for mayor, he had sworn to "consider the interests of the common people. If a thing is right, I will support it; if it is wrong, I will oppose it.... If I ever throw my weight the other way, I hope you'll tie a weight around me and throw me in the Bay. There are far too few champions of labor. We will need more as time goes on." As time went on, Mayor Lawrence's support of unionism and his refusal to call on outside police to break the Stelco picket line gave strikers the margin they needed to carry the strike to victory.

## THE FIRST DAY

Picket lines went up on Sunday, July 14, a day before the official start of the strike.

The strikers were jubilant at first. Reality sobered them fast. Two days later, Frank Malloy, one of the 2,700 strikers, drew back as strikebreakers, their faces blackened in commando-style, dashed through the gate and began clearing timber that had been stacked on railway tracks to block the trains from hauling steel. "Come on, boys. Clean it up," one shouted.

"Then everything broke loose," Malloy recalled. "I saw club-wielding company men leap from the flat cars and start slugging the strikers. I estimated 300 poured off the flat cars. Some had nice new pickaxe handles, which I had seen in the company storerooms. Others had heavy pieces of chain, long iron bolts, pieces of pipe, iron bars and bricks from the open hearth."

"Vimy Ridge was quiet compared to the half hour we had," striker David Borthman insisted. The allusion to the First World War battle site was appropriate. For the employers, 1946 was war.

## BRINGING IN SUPPLIES

Under the watchful eye of security staff, company men (except one at the right) scurried to unload supplies for the Stelco fortress.

The strike split families and friends. The men who stayed on the job called themselves "The Loyal Order of Scabs."

Strikers were embittered. "You can bet your life you'll be blacklisted," one striker wrote to a friend on the inside. "I never dreamed my old pal would scab, and when I walk past you anytime in the future, as dozens of your friends will, don't expect to be recognized. Your only chance to gain a little respect would be to get out now. Jump the fence and join your buddies fighting the masters."

The union asked all strikers to welcome these men into the union after the strike was over. But bad feelings continued to exist for many years to come.

## BY SEA AND AIR

Company arrogance prompted bold union tactics. The picket line was extended onto the water and into the skies. Ex-navy men took over the Whisper, a legendary speed launch from the rum-running days of the 1920s. The Whisper raced across Hamilton Bay, challenging shipments of men and supplies to the strikebound plant. After skirmishes with company vessels led to injuries and arrests on the union side, harbour authorities seized the speedy craft.

The strikers let fly against company stubbornness. Ernie Taylor, a veteran of the Atlantic Ferry Command, flew a small rented plane over the Stelco compound. At times, a bigger company plane engaged Taylor in mock dog-fight. Undaunted, he completed his mission, "bombing" the plant with leaflets and passes that read: "This man must be given free passage from the plant through the picket line at the east or west gates of Stelco. He wants to go home. Please assist him to reach there quickly."

## CROSSING THE T's

A sense of the ridiculous helped pass the time on picket duty. Years after the strike, former union president Alf Ready still cherished one burlesque incident which highlighted the new-found dignity of plant workers.

Anyone who went into the plant had to get a letter of permission from the union. "We had an old guy who was on the picket gate, and it was his job to examine any letter. This old guy would stop the supervisor, his own boss, every morning and say: 'Where are you going, sir? Have you any identification?' And the super would reach into his pocket and pull out the letter. Then, like the town crier, the old guy would read it aloud: 'To whom it may concern...,' dotting every i and crossing every t. He'd read everything, fold up the letter, hand it back and open the door. This went on every day.

## OUT OF THE WOODWORK

"When things happen like a strike," one Westinghouse union leader reminisced, "you ask: where does the personnel come from? They came out of the woodwork." When Westinghouse summarily rejected union demands for 25 cents an hour and a 44 hour work week, the rank and file sprang into action to organize picket duties, welfare emergencies and publicity.

"Not even the Ford strike at Windsor last fall saw such a galaxy of union loudspeakers," the Toronto *Star* gasped. "They urged the 'sisters and brothers' to make good and sure nobody got into either the east or west plant." Two thousand pickets massed on the east plant gate while 1,000 closed the entrance to the west entrance.

## UNION GUSTO

Picketers lined up for a spaghetti feast sponsored by the Italian community.

Italian and Italo-Canadian workers backed the strike to a man (and woman). Although many held back from joining the union before 1945, former union steward Tony Gervasio recalled, they "were out on strike immediately....Italians are temperamental people, and when you get their backs up, they go wholehearted at it."

They had special reasons to "get their backs up," for Stelco had long humiliated and demeaned them. Stelco assigned them to the hottest and dirtiest jobs that were considered "nigger work" in the United States. In order to get hired for these jobs, Gervasio remembered, "some of the foremen were paid off with whisky or something.... It was said to you all the time: 'There's a hundred more dagoes at the gate, anytime you don't like it.'" This abuse became even more intense when Canada and Italy declared war. Canadian-born and immigrant Italians alike were harassed and demoted.

## THE AUXILIARY

A women's auxiliary set up shop right at Stelco's main gate, where Mary Fiori ladled out soup for picketers.

"We had a kind of production line," auxiliary leader Betty Shipperbottom remembered. "We had a great big long table, and one lady went along and put a slice of bread down, and then another lady followed up with butter, and another would follow up with meat, then another slice of bread. Another did the cutting and packed them in boxes."

Women's support was crucial to the success of the strike, Mrs. Shipperbottom insisted.

Respect had to be earned the hard way though. "There's an awful lot of men who don't like women's organizations in their clubs," Mrs. Shipperbottom continued, with a flash in her eye. "It's a man's club and they want to keep it a man's club... Only, the men couldn't make the sandwiches and coffee and go on like we did, so they had to call on us. So there's another case of how they couldn't do without women.

"I know I had a run-in with one man, and he said he didn't like the idea of women coming in because they spoiled every union that was. So I said: 'If you think that, we'll back out right now.' The next thing, the strike came, and they were glad we were there. I didn't make him eat his words, but he ate a lot of sandwiches!"

## SOLIDARITY

Strikers could not live on picket lines alone, but their determination inspired generosity in others.

Families were going hungry, Alf Ready remembered, "and we didn't have much money. Then somebody donated a big dumptruck and we went out to the market gardeners in the Burlington area, and in an area kown as Czech Lane. One farmer gave a whole truckload of cabbage. Somebody gave forty baskets of tomatoes. There was one old lady who gave half a crate of eggs every week. Some person had a few pigs — he killed one, and gave us ten pounds of lard. We brought the stuff into the city, and the people went wild." Here, a UE volunteer crew picked up some of the donations.

"I think a great lesson was learned there," Ready continued, "by our people anyway, of how these people had given of themselves when they had nothing. It was loyalty to their fellow man."

## UNION MAESTRO

For 81 days, the strike tapped the resources of union supporters. Amateur entertainers, like the accordion player here, volunteered their talents to help pass time on the line.

Professional musicians performed as well, including Pete Seeger, and Woodie Guthrie who was backed up by his young son. Whipper Billy Watson and the Sharp Brothers provided an evening of wrestling for thousands who crowded into the Scott Park baseball stadium. All proceeds went to the union.

Most of this entertainment was offered at no cost, explained Bill Scandlan, a Canada Works employee in charge of recreation. It "sure took the drabness out of a strike," and kept up interest "when there wasn't any activity or any excitement going."

## PEOPLE'S PARK

Thousands gathered at Woodlands Park to catch the latest news on the strikes' progress.

The park had served as stamping grounds for working class activists since at least the 1930s. After the strike the city uprooted the park's majestic trees and destroyed its character. "No doubt, the strikes of 1946 helped to inspire the powers that be to cut down the trees and mutilate the park so that no large gathering could be held there," union electrician Bert McClure suggested.

## TAKING ON THE KING

King, Henderson and Hilton were knocked out with ridicule when they growled and doubletalked their way through the streets on Labour Day. The prickly legs carrying Norah Frances Henderson belonged to Murray Thomson, a Westinghouse production worker and amateur artist who created the effigies.

In mocking the alliance between big business and government, the strikers dramatized something of their own political understanding, fighting spirit, humour and artistic flair. In 1946, they marshalled these qualities, they took on the king, and they won.

## ONE YEAR LATER

Only the *Spectator* printers were left in the cold after 1946 but pickets kept the *Spectator's* headache throbbing when they celebrated "one year on the line."

According to the June, 1947 edition of their own newspaper, the *Classified News*, the strikers were more resolved than ever "to carry on the struggle until fair dealing under a closed shop union contract prevails in the *Spectator* and the Southam plants across the Dominion." The strikers' initiative and co-operation in publishing their own paper was reminiscent of a spirit that had not died with nineteenth century artisans.

Other craft traditions did not prove so helpful.

In this first Canadian strike between a craft union and a unified newspaper chain, unionized pressmen voted to abide by their contract with the company rather than honour the strike of fellow craftsmen. This doomed the printers' bid to stand up to the Southam chain and the dispute dragged on into the 1950s when the printers finally gave up.

# PHOTO CREDITS

Dominion Foundries & Steel Ltd. (Dofasco)
Marion Priest
Greening Donald Co.Ltd.
Dundas Historical Museum
Stelco Inc.
Brown Boggs Foundry and Machine Co. Ltd.
Public Archives of Canada (P.A.C.)
Leonard Hutchinson
Imperial Tobacco
Superior Engravers Ltd.
Art Gallery of Hamilton
Jim McCallum
Province of Ontario, Sessional Papers
Westinghouse Canada Ltd.
Slater Steel Industries Ltd.
Hamilton Public Library, Special Collections
International Harvester Canada
Bell Canada, Telephone Historical Collection
Head of the Lakes Historical Society
Joseph Brant Museum
The Multicultural History Society of Ontario
Lloyd Bloom
Charles Doubrough
Mr. J. Firth
Eaton's of Canada Ltd. Archives
Firestone Canada Inc.
National Steel Car Corp. Ltd.
Ernie Sims
Rev.M. Bailey
Jake Isbister
Mr.& Mrs. Jim English

Hamilton Street Railway
Mrs. Sadie Levy
Roy Burrows
Charles Doubrough
Mr. and Mrs. E. Morgan
J. Stewart
James Collection, City of Toronto Archives
Procter and Gamble Co. of Canada Ltd.
Mrs.Raye Lebow

Province of Ontario, Sessional Papers
Ontario Archives
United Electrical Workers of America, Local 504
*The Globe and Mail*
Head of the Lakes Historical Society
St. Anthony's Church
Barbara Reeves
Bob Newton
Mrs. H. Pomeroy
Archives, Mills Memorial Library, McMaster
University (Local 1005, U.S.W.A. Collection)
School of Nursing Archives, Hamilton Civic Hospitals

Thanks for special help to these individuals, not otherwise mentioned, at corporate and public sources

Walter Dunn . . . . . . . . . . . . . . . . . . . . . . . . Dofasco
Olive Newcombe . . . . . Dundas Historical Museum
Lou Heaton . . . . . . . . . . . Greening Donald Co. Ltd.
Don Andrew
Tim Kenyon
Jerry Little . . . . . . . . . . . . . Superior Engravers Ltd.
Joy Williams . . . National Photography Collection,
                                    Public Archives of Canada
Helen Hadden
Dan Thorburn . . . . . . . . . Art Gallery of Hamilton
Brian Henley . . . . . . . . . . . Hamilton Public Library
Mike Mackrory
Ruth Haverstock
George Newell . . . . . . . Westinghouse Canada Ltd.
Frank Cooke . . . . . . . . . . . Hamilton Street Railway
Elmer Moore . . . . . . . . . Slater Steel Industries Ltd.
Edward Laba
Angela Chung-Tack . . . . . . International Harvester
Shirley Hartt . . . . . . . . . . . . . Joseph Brant Museum
Joe Barbera . . . . . . . . . . . . . . Firestone Canada Ltd.
Gord Whiteman . . . . National Steel Car Corp. Ltd.
Harry Sisler . . . . . . . . National Steel Car Corp. Ltd.
Garry Smith . . . . . . . . . . . . . . . . . . . . . . . Stelco Inc.
Bruce Dawson . . . . . . . .    Procter and Gamble Co.
Peter Hill . . . . . . . . . . . . Hamilton Civic Hospitals